JOE AND I

LYLE CONAWAY

NEWMAN SPRINGS PUBLISHING
320 Broad Street
Red Bank, NJ 07701

First originally published by Newman Springs Publishing 2019

ISBN 978-1-64531-362-5 (Paperback)
ISBN 978-1-64531-363-2 (Digital)

Printed in the United States of America

*Dedicated
to those who
gave their
all in war.*

The Korean War (1950-1953)
saw the Corps expand from
75,000 regulars to a force of 261,000 Marines,
mostly reservists.
30,544 Marines were killed or wounded
during the war and 42 were awarded the Medal of Honor.

CHAPTER 1

I, Lyle Conaway, joined the Third Platoon, Fox Company, sometime in March 1951. I saw Joe Vittori often. He and his buddies stood out. He hung around with three Italians from Second Platoon who were very clannish. They were from the New York area—big guys, and I always thought I would not want to tangle with them. There were two other Italian guys there who, like Joe, were outgoing and friendly. One was a New York cop, and the other was an admitted car thief. It was comical listening to them razz each other.

In April 1951, we were sent up to plug a hole in the line that the Army and ROK (Republic of Korea) forces left when they fled in front of a major Chinese assault. At one point, we were surrounded and had to pull back across the river, which was very high and fast at that time because the Chinese had opened the floodgates on the Hwachon Reservoir Dam. Joe and I, with our Browning Automatic Rifles, (BARs) teamed up and were preventing the Chinese from coming at our flank, up through a concrete-lined drainage ditch. We hit several of them. Down the road which the ditch paralleled, up against a steep cliff of rock where the road turned, was a North Korean with a heavy machine gun firing in our general direction, harassing us and especially tough on anyone who had to cross the road.

We would elevate our BAR mortar-style and try to hit him, but the bullets' impact, noticeable by the dust kicking up, was so scattered that we could only hope for a hit.

They tried getting him with mortars but could not spend that much time concentrating on that one North Korean because of the masses of Chinese coming off the mountain to our front, just out of small arms reach. Orders at that time were to hold rifle fire until they get in range, watch the flanks. The airplanes were strafing and napalming the Chinese troops coming off the hills like ants. It did not slow them down.

At one point, they sent out an F4U Corsair to try to get the machine gunner who, when he ran out of a belt, had another Chinese appear from the ditch and run out. They set up the belt of ammo and ran back into hiding, leaving the machine gunner on his own. Then the Corsair came down the road on our right, hugging the road as close as he dared—actually he was flying below the altitude we were at on the mountainside. We could look across into the cockpit. Well, he came in with guns blazing, pulled up because of the high ground behind the gunner, and loosed a napalm bomb. We stood there, expecting to see one charred little slope-head. The smoke and dust cleared and, as though nothing had taken place out of the ordinary, there he still sat; he himself in the same place as before spitting out lead! We had to just figure "piss on 'im."

Not long after, the Chinese started putting the pressure on and were coming in range of our small arms. Then something took place that must have been in their planning. The wind was blowing toward us, and suddenly I saw a donkey go racing across the field with a burning bundle of straw on a rope behind it, setting the dry grass on fire. The smoke became really thick, burning our eyes and choking our breathing, with the Chinese coming behind it like in an old western movie. By this time, they were starting up the hills toward where we were. I would look down the hill at them from time to time to see where they were, while with Joe and a few others we were still watching our flank and firing to prevent them from coming up the ditches.

Soon people started filing past us down across the road and up the hill on the other side. We quickly realized we were the rear guard when we could hear the Chinese shouting commands and blowing whistles, really making us even more uncomfortable. Finally, we heard our guys shouting from across the road for us to get out of there and follow them up the opposite hill. The bullets now were going through the trees by the thousands and making crackling and whizzing, zinging sounds accompanied by shouts and whistles.

We all let go with long bursts of automatic fire, and the machine guns on the opposite hill were firing over our heads. Everyone turned to run but leave it to me; I couldn't do it right. Instead of going around a bunker that was covered with sandbags, I decided to jump on top and over it. When my foot came down on top of the bunker, the roof collapsed, and through the roof I went—one leg inside the bunker and the other on top. When I struggled to get myself out, the sandbags broke, and suddenly I was inside the bunker up to my chest. No one saw this, and it did no good to shout; no one except the Chinese would have heard me. I had to lay my BAR down on solid ground and then kept struggling—panicking now because the North Koreans were so close. I could smell the garlic. This was the first of three times in my Korean experience that I thought, for sure, I would be killed or taken prisoner; a fate worse than death. I was frantically tearing at the sandbags, trying to get them open. Finally, the sand fell to the bunker floor, giving me a few more inches to stand on, and by grabbing some tree roots, I managed to crawl out. But I was totally exhausted to the point that I didn't even duck the bullets anymore.

Across the road, they discovered I was missing, and Joe and Newberry came back to the road. When they saw me, they started firing into the trees behind me and shouting for me to run. Fortunately, the road was downhill, so I could kind of run, stumbling like a drunken Irishman. And I got across. Joe and Newberry both grabbed me and helped me the first twenty feet up the hill. Everyone was tired. Still, we made it to the top with bullets striking all around. I must mention that Lt. Harry Randall was on top of making sure his platoon was accounted for. I had been told earlier that Joe Vittori was a guy you could count on in a tight spot—I now knew it for certain.

We made it up the hill and into new positions, where we expected an attack that night. Around midnight, it was unusually quiet in our sector when, suddenly, one of our machine guns opened up with a brief exchange of fire to my left. When morning came we discovered a platoon or so of Chinese had come up one of the spines that was covered by a machine gun operated by Corporal Craddok, a reservist who in civilian life was a schoolteacher in California. The North Koreans came in toward him and evidently did not know where they were as they were not being too cautious. Craddok, waiting for the BARs that flanked him to open up, realized when the Chinese were twenty-five to thirty yards away that he would have to do it himself. As he was lining up on them, one suddenly stood up in the open and gave a command of some sort. Several more came walking out of the brush, knelt down, laid a map on the ground, took out a flashlight, and were looking at the map with their asses in the air. Within fifteen seconds, they were all dead, still kneeling over the map. Craddok did some beautiful shooting.

The next day is not clear in my memory until toward evening. We had been guarding a concrete bridge. There were trucks and tanks and wounded and mortar and all kinds of activity going on across the river about a hundred feet or so below us. Just before dark, I saw an army unit cross the bridge and load into trucks with what seemed to me considerable apprehension. The trucks drove off. There was a lot of fighting going on some distance from us on both sides. I guess they were trying to surround us to save the bridge.

We weren't really paying much attention to all the activity across the river and behind us until late in the afternoon when a couple rocket launching trucks fired two missions of rockets right behind us, scaring the shit out of everyone. Then the rocket launching trucks scurried out, and we got a shit pot full of incoming mortars. Shortly after that, we were informed by a sergeant that, as soon as all the army equipment was across the bridge, they are going to blow the bridge. We would then have the honor of crossing that raging river on a rope that was stretched from the base of a large pine tree to a tank across the river. The tank had been backed up to put tension on the rope, which then was reduced in size so that we could grip it.

Someone cleverly asked, "Why the hell do we have to cross on a rope?" The bridge was still there.

The answer was "Because you're Marines! Shut up about it, and don't let go of that rope. Or your ass will be floating somewhere out in the Sea of Japan!" Shortly after that, they blew the bridge.

So we crossed after dark—hand over hand, lying prone, stretched out straight by the rushing, cold water, with all our equipment on our bodies—and we lost no one. As we were getting into the water, all in high spirits, I was thinking, *If only I could hear the Marine Corps hymn.*

That night, we walked through the Chinese lines having been warned not to smoke, to keep quiet, and whatever else, do not swear. They didn't pay much attention to us. We walked all night, our feet raw with blisters, but we made it. Once there, we rested for a couple weeks.
So ended April 1951.

Marine Corps Hymn

From the Halls of Montezuma
To the Shores of Tripoli;
We fight our country's battles
In the air, on land and sea;
First to fight for right and freedom
And to keep our honor clean;
We are proud to claim the title
of United States Marine.

Our flag's unfurled to every breeze
From dawn to setting sun;
We have fought in ev'ry clime and place
Where we could take a gun;
In the snow of far-off Northern lands
And in sunny tropic scenes;
You will find us always on the job
The United States Marines.

Here's health to you and to our Corps
Which we are proud to serve
In many a strife we've fought for life
And never lost our nerve;
If the Army and the Navy
Ever look on Heaven's scenes;
They will find the streets are guarded
By United States Marines.

CHAPTER 2

I cannot remember how May went by, but I know we were on the lines for a couple of weeks because I remember writing a letter home to my friends in the Marmas Bar, informing them that I turned 21-years-old on that day, May 8, 1951. It seems we came back in reserve for a short time. We were angry because the North Koreans broke through the army's lines again, and we again had to go up and plug the hole.

While we were in the reserve area, we noticed far more helicopter and air activity, and we could hear artillery pounding steadily. We would watch the choppers on their return trips, and if we saw blankets flapping around the edges of the body pods on the sides of the copters, we knew they were carrying wounded. Then the breakfast of steak and eggs, and no one had to tell you to "roll up your equipment—you're moving out."

Sometime in May, Lieutenant Randall asked me if I thought the men would like to have R&R. I asked what R&R was, and he stated that we would go to Japan for one week by air and live it up and then come back.

I replied, "And then come back?" The lieutenant nodded *yes*.

I told him, "Lieutenant, I speak for myself, but once I leave this place, I ain't never coming back!" No more was ever said on the subject.

On June 3, 1951, about 0700 hours, we had the usual air strikes and artillery barrages and then began our assault, accompanied by tanks on a hill in the area of what was called the Punch Bowl. We started up the ridgeline on both sides with our tanks firing at bunkers and other targets and in between our lines, which were fifteen feet apart. Those tanks were marvelous—if they could see a target, they could hit it. I saw one bunker they hit. In it was a North Korean who was cut clean in half. The bottom half was sitting in one corner with legs crossed and the upper torso sitting to the right of it, looking almost bewildered at its lower half. When the tanks could no longer support us, we had to start checking the bunkers ourselves. One man would walk or crawl, whichever method worked best, while two men covered.

While Captain Groff and the lieutenant briefly discussed something, I sat out of breath, resting, and noticed three figures walking on the ridgeline about 300 yards away. In my tired stupor, I did not realize they were North Koreans.

Suddenly the captain yelled, "Get those bastards! Shoot them! Shoot them!" I jumped up to take aim. When I brought the BAR up, my pack pushed my helmet down over my eyes. The captain was still shouting, "Shoot! Shoot!" I flipped my helmet off onto the ground, aimed high, led them, and fired. I don't think I hit them, but they sure ducked in a hurry. No slap on the back for that one.

The lieutenant then told Sgt. Smith from Ogden, Utah, to take Conaway and check the rest of the bunkers. There were four or five between us and the top of the hill. I fired into the first one, and Smith ran up and dropped a grenade in it. The next three were the same. The last one, on the very crest of the hill, was a larger bunker which looked quite abandoned, so Smitty was just walking up to it and did not indicate he wanted me to fire. I had my BAR across my body and was briefly distracted by some members of the Second Platoon who were swearing at our guys for firing on them. Suddenly, three grenades exploded right in front of Smitty, lifting him into the air, and striking me in the left hand and into my BAR. I hit the deck, diving into a shallow shell hole, next to a log. The muzzle of a machine gun poked through the slot in the bunker and started firing. I was so close I could feel the muzzle blast. I came up to fire, hoping to hit them good enough to get out of there. I came up and raised my BAR to fire, and nothing happened. My damn BAR was jammed! Now the assistant gunner in the bunker, feeding the belt into the gun, saw me, tapped the gunner, and pointed at me. The gunner tried to lower the gun enough to hit me but a burst of fire across the face of the bunker forced him to start firing again at the guys behind me. One of them was Joe. I lay behind the log long enough to see that I was being ignored. I looked at my BAR and saw it was clogged with dirt. After quickly digging the dirt out with my fingers, I saw that the bolt would go home. Hoping to act before one of them used another grenade or weapon to get me, I came up in front of them and let go a burst that flattened those bastards. I scurried to the rear of the bunker, feeling pretty cocky, and tossed a grenade. It entered the bunker and finished the job.

Unbeknownst to me, when I came up to fire, I came up right in front of Joe, who was just going to squeeze off a burst. (When I got back from the hospital thirty days later, I was told by Sgt. Smith that Joe told him that he damn near got me. Joe never mentioned it to me.)

When I got back behind some cover, there were the lieutenant and sergeant. The lieutenant was shouting to the rear and motioning for a machine gun to come up. He had his .45 in his hand. The captain came walking up to the lieutenant, disregarding the lead that was whistling all around, and told Lieutenant Randall, "Harry, put that pistol away before you shoot someone with it." The corpsman who was bandaging my hand, me, and Newberry, who had been shot through the shoulder, could see the lieutenant was embarrassed, so we pretended we didn't hear the captain's order. Still standing, the captain went on to explain to Lieutenant Randall why he wanted a rocket instead of a machine gun. Because the captain was standing, Lieutenant Randall was required to remain standing, though he did so very reluctantly.

I was given credit for destroying the bunker and awarded a Navy Commendation Medal.

Ah, but getting to the hospital! After being wounded, I went down to the base of the hill with Newberry and the other walking wounded to where the tanks were. There was a North Korean who was crawling around on his hands and knees, going up to people and calling for a doctor. From his looks, I believe he had typhus. We ignored him for the time being. I did not want him close to me and made that clear to him. I think they called in helicopters for the other two guys and loaded me and the North Korean in a six-by truck.

Somewhere along the line, I got dropped off, and it started to rain. I was laid on a stretcher and covered with a poncho. At the time, I thought to myself I was glad it was just because of the rain that I had been covered. I wasn't dead and wasn't in a wet, sloppy foxhole.

Next, a jeep with a frame to carry four stretchers stopped. I was put on the jeep with three others lying there. We were all covered with ponchos to keep the rain off. When I lifted the edge of the poncho and peeked out, I noticed that one of the other men on a stretcher did not have shoes on, and his feet were yellowish looking with scars from blisters that made the scars understandable. In a very rough manner, they strapped me to the jeep. The drive was also really rough, but I figured that, if no one else was complaining, I would also endure it. After a few miles, the jeep stopped, and I looked out again by lifting the edge of the poncho to prevent getting wet from the continuing rain. I noticed about twenty stretchers lying outside and a row of tents to the left. We were unloaded, and the jeep drove off. I lay there for a while, listening to the rain on the poncho and the sounds of people in the background, content to be out of combat and not climbing those damn hills. Finally, I heard someone speaking. I looked out and saw a chaplain kneeling about three stretchers down from where I was. Still not concerned, I waited until he got to me and then said, "Hello, chaplain." He almost shit, stuttered without getting a word out, then turned and shouted toward the tents. Two men came running out and he told them, "Get this man inside!" Then he turned to me and apologized profusely. It still took a while to register with me that I was at a graves registration unit, where I was the only live soul on a stretcher. I was finally transferred to Easy Medical Battalion where I received excellent care.

In the hospital, we were on cots inside of tents. They dug the piece of shrapnel from my hand. I was resting with about ten to twelve others when, suddenly, what seemed like machine gun fire erupted right outside. Everyone bailed off their cots onto the floor, tubes and all. The commotion was a helicopter landing alongside the tent.

Quick reactions from all of us—we were at that stage where any sharp sound caused us to duck.

While in the hospital, I would go out to the main service road and catch rides with the truckers who were more than willing to have company, especially guys from the lines so they could use our stories and write home about our adventures. About midnight, after visiting a Dutch unit a couple of miles up the road, I got a ride with a South Korean supply truck. The driver could speak no English, but when we approached a supply depot, which was about three blocks from the hospital area, he indicated to me he was turning left into the depot. Not giving it a thought, I stepped out of the truck to start back to the hospital while he showed his credentials to the guard. The truck pulled away, and I was facing a very startled Korean guard who held a very real carbine rifle. With a shout of something that sounded like "oongao," he brought the rifle up, cocked it and shouted something else.

Again, and this was becoming a frequent event with me, my heart was in my throat, and I immediately did something very commendable on my part. I threw my hands up, and he shouted another order. I said, in the calmest voice I could muster, "I'm an American Marine."

He answered in perfect English, "I am sorry." He lowered his rifle and smiled as though nothing happened.

I pretended I wasn't bothered by the incident and said, "That's okay," and turned and walked away as well as my rubbery legs would allow.

So ended June '51 with me in the hospital.

CHAPTER 3

About July 1, I returned to my unit, which was dug in trench warfare style, on what they called the Kansas Line. Not much was happening. Just a few probing attacks, a lot of patrols, some mortar, harassing fire and a lot of boredom.

On one patrol, we had to go through thick forest and down a steep incline to a very well kept, wide gravel road. We crossed this road and went up the ridges on the other side, where we knew we were in North Korean country. We could feel them watching us. On one occasion, I somehow acquired some field glasses, and during a break, I said to whoever was there that I thought I'd take a look at some North Korean looking at us. I put the glasses to my eyes, and there in front of us, about half way up the hill, were three North Koreans, picking stuff out of a garden, right near where our patrols would end. Assured of what I was looking at, I hurried ahead and found the lieutenant who I informed in a stage whisper what I had observed—but it was old news. The lieutenant knew they were there and was in fact calling in mortars on them. I think we got one of them as they ran for cover, apparently warned by someone who saw our patrol.

One morning before dawn, we heard one of the mines go off down on the road to our left. When daylight came, we saw a Korean civilian, sitting beside his cow that had stepped on a land mine.

During this relatively uneventful period, I invented an imaginary Chinese soldier/spy who was constantly crawling up under cover of dark or in the brush and grass, listening to our conversations, reports, and orders. I named him Private Puska Housut, which, in Finnish, means "shit pants." For example, if we had the patrol the next morning, the lieutenant would come out of the bunker and tell the platoon sergeant to let the men know they have patrol at 0500 hours. My bunker was on the forward slope opposite the lieutenant's, and I would warn, "Uh-oh, Lieutenant. Well, it's too late now. Puska Housut heard that, and he's on his way with the news." Sometimes you'd do anything to break the monotony.

One day, Easy Company was on patrol, and they ran into an ambush, which had no real serious consequences. I was standing near the ridgeline where we left and returned into the lines. One of the Easy Company men said, "Puska Housut must have told them we were coming." On another patrol, they did not get in until after dark, and the password was *George Washington*. There was a guy who stuttered when he became excited, so when the first guys came through, they said that Private B was the rear guard.

The rear guard consisted of two men who had to sit, one on each side of the column, and count the number of men returning in the column. For instance, if you went out with twelve men and came back with thirteen, there was, you might say, a North Korean in the woodpile. Well, when the rear guard came up to the machine gun at the line, the gunners asked for the password.

Probably not able to remember on the spur of the moment, Private B replied, "W-w-we're t-t-the r-r-rear guard." The gunner stated that he didn't care who he says he was; he wanted the password. So, Private B stuttered out "G-G-G-G." Then he heard the guys laughing, and yelled, "F-f-f— ya, go-go ahead and shoot!"

During this time of year in Korea, it was mating season for coo-coo birds, and for a couple of weeks, there was coo-cooing all over the countryside. It became a serious military problem for a while. Some guys actually had to be treated for nervous conditions because of this. Several times I heard someone shout, "You son of a bitch, shut the f— up!" Then a burst from a BAR or rifle. You'd see the top fall off the tree, and a couple seconds later, there was the *coo-coo, coo-coo*. It prompted an order to be issued stating that anyone firing at the coo-coo birds would be court martialed.

I remember one afternoon some poor stressed-out chap shouted out, "I don't care if they do court martial me." Then he let a burst from a Thompson gun go, knocking branches off a pine tree. You just heard silence and the echo of the burst through the valley below.

Shortly, there was the inevitable *coo-coo-coo-coo* and someone saying, "Get that man down to the CP."

Some of the sayings and slang of the day were directed at the president like "Harry-assed Truman" or "Harry's Hillside Cops." Other phrases were "Pardon me for living," "Take a f— at a rolling doughnut," "Suchahatchi," "Your mother wears combat boots." "From out of the Korean mountains comes the cry of the hatchet bird—cutcha cockoff—cutcha cockoff."

Someone would shout out, "Who will carry the mail to Hamhung?"

And the exchange would be on "Sir, wounded tho' I am, I will carry the mail." "How old are you son?" "76 sir." "That's the spirit."

Our battalion: Second Battalion, First Regiment, Fox or F Company, was on the line sixty-two days. It was not really as hazardous as other times or areas because there were no big pushes during this time by either side. The so-called peace talks were taking place. What really happened was that we allowed those sneaky bastards time to do what they did so well, dig into the ground with trenches, bunkers and tunnels. And we were about to pay for that. Our danger seemed to be in our own camp. We had constructed bunkers with trees cut for us by Korean laborers and then stacked sandbags around and on top of them. Some of the guys with no knowledge of how much weight there was on top of the structures were crushed or suffocated when they collapsed during the rains.

Sometime in August, we were relieved by army troops whose highest concern was our bug-out route. This referred to our trench and bunker systems, which they could use to escape when attacked. That really pissed us off—that damned army was a disgrace.

A sergeant standing nearby stated, in an angry and insulting manner, "You bastards haven't even got in position yet, and you're thinking of retreating. We're getting tired of having to come out of reserve to save you yellow bastards. The next time we have to come back up because you can't hold a position, I'm going to start shooting any f—ing doggie I see headed south with no weapons. I'll take a court martial."

Those army personnel did not say a word in defense of that statement; they knew it was the truth. It was not the fault of the individual army personnel. They lacked the training at that time. The army and navy did not envision combat. In fact, they never thought another war was possible five years after the last terrible war ended. Posters read, "Join the Army. Travel. Drive a Truck. Learn a Trade." The Navy posters said, "Join the Navy. See the World." The Marines, on the other hand, stated, "This Rifle Needs a Man."

I remember reading of an incident that took place in the early part of the war when the army was a complete shambles and small, platoon-sized groups were trying to get back to safety—abandoning the wounded, the dead, and equipment, artillery, tanks, everything. A unit was dug in along a road as darkness came on when one of the men called to the lieutenant.

"Appears to be a platoon-sized group of soldiers coming our way down the road. We cannot identify them as friend or foe. What are the orders?"

Probably very tired and very unstable in every respect, the lieutenant said, "If they appear to be organized, fire on them—they can't be ours."

So off the hill we came in the rain, sliding and tumbling on the greasy path made by hundreds of people—dirty, smelly, sore, tired, but happy as could be. We were going to the rear for rest. And it was truly a rest—one of the most memorable times of relaxation and good times we experienced as a unit—the lull before the storm.

CHAPTER 4

About the middle of August, we went into reserve in an area alongside a wide river, but I don't remember its name. It was also alongside the main service road. We in Fox Company were assigned to an area that was partly rice paddy with some mounds and small hills. When we arrived there were dead North Koreans lying everywhere. It appeared to me they may have been caught in the open by aircraft. A corporal was operating a D8 Caterpillar, blading the area and covering the bodies. Before I was called back to active duty in September of 1950, I had been working in the iron mines for Cleveland Cliffs Iron Company operating heavy equipment, especially D8 Dozers. When I mentioned this to my comrade, I had the feeling they did not believe me like I was too young to be trusted with $100,000 machines.

Well, I flagged down the dozer driver, got up on the track, told him I was experienced in operating this machine, and then begged him to let me make a couple passes with it. I explained how much prestige it would give me, with all the guys watching. He very reluctantly and nervously allowed me to take over as he sat on the arm of the seat while I made two passes, back-blading the spot he was working on. After covering many bodies with a thin layer of soil and pretty well leveling the tent area, the Cat was used to dig out a trench the width of the blade and about three feet deep. It was then lined with a large tarp, and we were instructed to throw all our grenades and ammo onto the tarp, except for one clip per rifle. The tarp was then covered over tent fashion to keep it dry.

In spite of all the Cat skinner's efforts (a salty reference to a dozer operator), when he left the area there was right in the middle of what turned out to be the company street, a corpse lying on his back, spread-eagle, with a hole in the top of his head. It was covered with flies and was generally ignored by everyone. I thought it odd that someone wasn't detailed to bury it. But that was to come.

Starting the next day, we were deloused and showered down by the river. Then we had to wash our clothes and were given needles, thread, and patch material and were ordered to patch our clothing. Next, we stood inspection and if the patching was not acceptable we did it again. After that, we cleaned our gear and rifles and stood inspection again. Finally, we went down to a couple of large semi-trucks where they had the shoe and textile repair set up. We had our shoes half-soled and patched and stood inspection once more.

On about the third day, they gave us one final inspection, issued orders as to how to conduct ourselves and to not leave the area beyond the river, which we promptly ignored. Then, on that day, they gave us the treat of our military lives. *Beer!* About four cases each man, all different kinds of beer—Pabst, Bud, Schlitz, and more. Man was that great! The weather was beautiful, we were in good spirits, clean, good chow, and now, the nectar of the gods—or as our drill instructor in boot camp referred to it, Panther Piss. Needless to say, we tore into that without hesitation, and it wasn't long before we were singing, laughing, wrestling, and having one helluva time. Well, after several hours of partying, we started to crap out. One chap, who was in the tent where the dead North Korean lay, couldn't resist putting his foot on the swollen stomach and pushing it down, saying to him, "Wanna drink, gook?" (Slang for North Korean soldier during the war.)

When he put pressure on the stomach, a gush of yucky fluid came squirting out of the hole in the top of the head, which this chap found to be very amusing. So he shouted to the others, "Look here!" Once again, he applied pressure and *squish*. That's what the CO Captain Groff was waiting for. He called the guy over to the CP, gave him a shovel, and told him to bury that North Korean. That's extremely difficult to do when you're pissed up. Even that was entertainment. We were having one really good time like people go on vacations and camping trips for.

I was quite familiar with that area, having been hospitalized for a month at Easy Med down the road a way. And I knew there were women to be had back in those towns. When I told the guys that, they insisted I show them. I had been told and shown where the houses were—on a hill across the river from a black transport group, who treated me like royalty, gave me chow and whiskey, and asked me a hundred questions of what it was like up on the lines.

Meanwhile, we had all these cases of beer, which wouldn't last forever. Then, realizing that some of the other units had been in this area longer than we had, we figured their beer supply would be dwindling, and truthfully, some were on the prowl for beer. That's as bad as any communist invasion. Two or three guys would group rations together and would sleep on top of and around the stash. I can still vividly picture in my memory one chap, lying atop his ration, sleeping and snoring, passed out, with a Thompson machine gun lying across his body.

The mess tent at that time was on the opposite end of the company street from the CP and adjacent to our tent. The mess sergeant had a very good voice and early in the morning, since there was no reveille, he would sing light opera or classical songs, and it was very pleasing to all. About this time, especially early in the morning, I could smell from time to time the odor of decaying flesh. That wasn't uncommon in the warm weather, and I would ask Olie (Jervis D. Olson) and whoever was sacking on either side of me if they could smell the decay every morning. They more or less agreed that they could smell it sometimes.

I am not a religious person. I do believe there is a supreme power or god, but I never attended any of the religious gatherings they would have on Sunday. But I always liked the old hymns they sang, probably because it reminded me of when I was a child and was forced to attend a Baptist church where I learned at a very tender age that most of the elders, or whatever their titles were, were closet drinkers and were half-gassed when they would get up and launch into a tirade on how sinful the rest of the world is—with tears streaming and all—while they were fortified with a few Jack Daniels. But I did like the old hymns. I do not remember if Joe attended any of those gatherings, but I think not. Does it really matter?

During this time in reserve, I was relieved of the BAR, and I became a rifleman. We all liked the BAR when we were dug in, but there was about eleven pounds difference in weight. When I was given my rifle I was eager to try it out and familiarize myself with it. We called a sergeant the master at arms as he professed to know everything there was to know about firearms. He knew I wanted to fire it, so he suggested we take it out to an area he and I had visited a couple days before, where there was a Chinese 76 field piece sitting alongside a small pond. The pond was home to hundreds of red-belly frogs, and we had taken a case of grenades with us and blasted some of the frogs out of the water. So we gathered up a hundred rounds of ammo and walked out to this place for a little target practice.

After firing many rounds at various targets, I laid by the edge of the pond and dropped some more of the grenades we had left there into the water. Grenades in a couple feet of water are almost ineffective. While I was doing that, the sergeant removed the breech clock from the 76 and laid it down so that one of the four flat sides were facing him, mumbling something about disabling that cursed thing for good. So before I could make some suggestions, he pumped an armor-piercing round into the block, which was made of manganese steel, and I saw the flash of the bullet ricochet back past the sergeant's head. And I told him I saw that slug go. He stated that armor-piercing bullets do not ricochet and brought the rifle up again. I ducked down behind him. He fired. The slug came back and struck him in the wrist, damaging his wrist quite badly.

He threw the rifle up by reflex, grabbed his wrist, and yelled, "Oh shit, oh shit, oh that hurts. I didn't think that would happen." At first, we were trying to concoct a story that it was a booby trap but decided to just state that we were trying to permanently destroy an enemy gun. He was due to leave for the states anyway, so it worked out okay. I believe he even received a Purple Heart. I was never asked about it.

While drinking our beer ration, of course, we would reflect back on some of the happenings and, most of the time, mentioned only the lighter side. Like the time a new replacement was startled when a mortar round struck close to his hole. He jumped out of the hole, went in circles a couple times, jumped into another hole, and with wide eyes said, "They're using 180-millimeter mortarmeters!" Or the time they had some mules they took from the Chinese and a mortar round killed the mule and it fell on top of the guy when he was in a hole. When a couple of guys rushed over to pull the donkey off of him, he was trying to hold the donkey there shouting, "Leave it there, leave it there!"

One incident I remember well is the time Corporal Frank S. had about five guys make a purchase for him from a PX truck that came to the area. Each one bought a bottle of Aqua-Velva. You were allowed one each. Now the corporal had six, and he commenced to drink them and he got smashed. And he was telling stories about how he grew up in New York. It was interesting. Then he told of his two pet canaries and how they had been in cages for all these years. Now he was getting emotional, stating that after being in the cage himself for four years (meaning at this time, the Corps) he knew how those birds must feel, and one of the first things he would do when he got home would be to open the cage of one and tell the bird, "cutta-cutta," which is Korean for go-go. The other one he would leave in the cage because he was a gung ho bird as he sang all the time. He paid dearly for that drunk. He looked like shit for the next three days and smelled like a perfume factory.

We would also talk about how the newspapers would refer to the Chinese forces as being there in hordes. Hordes of Chinese Struck the UN Lines Today read the headlines. So when we would describe a fight, often someone would ask, "Were we fighting a horde?" Or if you described an area where you would have to patrol as having a lot of enemy, you would be asked, "Will there be hordes?"

One time they had a half-assed USO show, and all the girls were North Koreans. Any talent they may have possessed was not in the field of music. I don't remember how Sergeant Smith and I got around behind the stage, but with a few beers we felt a little frisky and started tickling these "performers" in the ass with a couple of twigs. Soon they were swearing at us and a drunken army lieutenant came rushing around behind and started chewing our butts out. After giving us hell, I stood at attention and said, "Yes, sir." And I saluted him. That surprised him so that he hesitated, not knowing what to do.

When he brought his hand up to return the salute, he became entangled in the tenting and couldn't move his arm freely, so Sergeant Smith rushed over to assist him. At the same time, he removed the bottle of whiskey the lieutenant had in his field jacket, slipping it under his own dungaree jacket. The lieutenant then somehow surmised that we had done him a favor and stated, "Okay, guys, go and enjoy the show." In spite of the show, we did enjoy the whiskey.

Sometimes, while standing in chow line, we had no mess kits. Most of us just carried a spoon in our dungaree jacket pocket, and when back in the rear, we would form paper plates from the cardboard the mess cooks threw out from the boxes the rations came in. On this particular day, we were supposed to keep our dungaree jackets buttoned up because some shit-head asshole army general was supposed to be inspecting the place. We were standing in chow line, and I did not have my dungaree jacket buttoned. I just forgot. Suddenly, from behind me, I got a swift kick right in the ass. I really felt it. In an instant, I became really angry. I dropped my eating utensils and turned to look at a staff sergeant who was about 5'10" or so. I did not care about his size. I'm only 5'8". Didn't care about his rank either. I just knew in that instant I could beat the piss out of that bastard. He backed up, paled a little, and muttered about my unbuttoned jacket.

I replied, "You son of a bitch!"

Three or four of my friends quickly shouted, "Don't do it, Connie. Don't do it!"

I stopped, glared at that bastard, and told him in front of everyone, "I won't forget this!" In all my years, I have never seen one big guy ever fight with another his size.

Anyway, I did not forget that incident. I had my few minutes of revenge later up on Hill 749, when we were catching some fire from a probing attack. I was going along a path, crouched down, and I saw this brave asshole down in a hole, cranking on a field phone. I seldom wore a helmet, so he recognized me when I stopped. I looked him right him in the eyes, stood up in spite of the fire, and—with my rifle pointed away from him—said, "Want to try it now, Sergeant?" I could see he was scared, so I just went on my way, knowing he would be wondering. I don't remember the name, or I would sure mention it. I never saw him again.

Another big guy we had with us was always put in charge of any detail he happened to be with like on the ship on the way over and back in the States as well. I never was directly involved with him but couldn't help noticing how important he thought he was. On a couple of occasions, I heard him make statements about how he was going to kick some ass and straighten a few of the shitheads up. The last I saw him was after one of our first engagements with small arms and grenades, etc. Two corpsmen, one on each arm, were leading him down a path as he was sobbing uncontrollably. When they came to a dead North Korean lying across the path, he stopped and started kicking it, shouting, "I'll kill you, you bastard. I'll kill you!" I heard later he became a chaplain's orderly.

Our time back in reserve went smoothly. On one occasion, Joe and I were bathing in the river. While in water about waist deep, I was bumped by something under water. I thought at first Joe had bumped me until I saw this body, with a bare upper torso, rolling along just under the surface. Joe and I watched it until it disappeared downstream. I felt dirtied and seemed I couldn't scrub enough.

Suddenly, something grabbed by ankles. I kicked and jumped, shouting something unintelligible. Then I saw it was Joe. Laughing as I attacked—it wasn't much of a match—and after being under water a few seconds, I calmed down, still cursing him even as he apologized.

One other incident, I recall happening while back in reserve. Our squad leader was a Tennessee ridgerunner named Weaver, who for the most part was okay. He sort of kept to himself, quiet, easy-going, until you added alcohol and he started reliving the Civil War. Then anyone north of the Mason-Dixon line was a damn Yankee. With a little more Panther Piss, we were goddamn Yankees.

Well, one late afternoon Weaver was really getting into the mood with some statements that were getting wilder as he went on. When he would say the damn Yankee uttering, he would always be looking in our direction—Olson and me from Minnesota and Hoover from Illinois. Weaver was a pretty husky sort (reminds me of the skinny guy who went to Alaska and came back a husky f'kr) about 5'8", with big round eyes and red hair. Not a handsome sort—maybe that's why he would get so nasty. Well, he raved on. He mentioned that when it came to slaughter the people who were up front were the boys from the south. And not only that. Yankees were just plain yellow, and he could lick any damn Yankee. Olie (Jervis D. Olson) from Minneapolis, Minnesota, was a semi-pro football player, about 6'4" and 220 pounds, with blond hair and ears that would slow him down in a good wind. Olie was an easy-going guy, really pretty scared in combat. Probably had more sense than some of us. But finally, Weaver yanked his chain, and Olson told him, "You f—ing blowhard ridgerunning hillbilly. Come on outside, and I'll kick your ass." Out they went.

It was one hell of a scrap. The whole company was out in the street watching. The captain, of course, had to pretend he was unaware of it taking place and stayed back in his tent. He too was a Stars and Bars Southerner who had the flag over his tent door. Olson finally got Weaver. It was one of the cleanest, most evenly matched fights I ever witnessed. Weaver would be reminded later on of his statement that only the Rebels were up front.

CHAPTER 5

The last couple days, we had noticed the helicopters bringing back a lot of casualties; we saw the blankets flapping on the pods. About September 9, we attended the evening movie, and Colonel Warnham got up on stage and told us, "I don't know for sure where we're going, but I know it will be soon. And I know there will be a lot of Purple Hearts. I know you won't let me down." We all stood up and sang the Marine Corps hymn with a lot of feeling.

The next morning, our beautiful little world in reserve came to an end. The guys came back from morning chow, shouting, "Start packin'."

I asked, "What's up?"

"Steak and eggs!" Okay, we all knew what that meant.

I mentioned earlier about every now and then, especially when there wasn't much breeze, that I would smell the dead North Koreans while others didn't seem bothered. Well, in packing up when I pulled my poncho up from the ground, I noticed I had to tug at it, and what a stench came up. Sticking to my poncho was soil that had been covering this dead North Korean, and when I stepped back a few feet, I could see the dark outline where the fluids had permeated the soil above and around it. That's where I had been getting an occasional odor. Now, when I think of it, maybe that cushion under my poncho provided a little more comfort, kind of like a posturepedic. I would have shit-canned the poncho, but there was nowhere else to get another one. So I had the mess cooks squirt some soapy water on it and went on my way. We struck the tents, policed the area, threw the debris into a pile and set it afire, then called roll.

We were issued helmets, rations, and ammo then held inspection. We were asked to carry as much ammo as we could. When standing in one spot you can load up pretty good with bandoliers, belts of ammo, grenades, and all, but half a mile down the road you start dumping. I shed my helmet first—I found it very encumbering. A helmet was always flopping and forever sliding down over my eyes when I fired my weapon. There would come a time I regretted not having one, but for the most part, I was comfortable without it. Others felt the same, Joe being one of them.

I cannot remember exactly how we got to the battalion assembly area, whether we walked all the way or if we rode some. Nor do I remember for sure the date. An educated guess would be September 11, 1951. We arrived at the assay area late in the afternoon. I remember a river forward of us, and I was looking at the base of Kanmubong Ridge and two other objectives we were to take. There was a spiny, low-profile ridge that appeared to be half-moon shaped and about twenty-five feet in height that we were up against. In fact, I was about halfway up this embankment looking things over. A radio jeep with the air Forward Observer (FO) was just below and about a hundred feet away. I could hear the air traffic on the jeep radio.

About 1700 hours, we suddenly received a round from a 76 (flat-trajectory gun). I do not know if it caused any casualties, but soon everyone was looking for somewhere to get out of the line of fire as several more rounds came whistling in. The air FO was frantically speaking to aircraft coordinators to get an air strike on that gun which, as with all 76 flat trajectory guns, showed a distinct flash when fired. I remember there was a twin peak appearance on top of the knot they were firing from, and the gun was just below that. I was in a fairly comfortable place on the side of that ridge but still could hear pieces of shrapnel from the rounds.

Two F4U Corsairs came on the scene, and the FO was giving them advice as to where the gun was situated. They would then make a pass to see if they could ID it. After a couple passes, one pilot reported that he had it, he'd mark it. Then down he went firing 20mm and rockets into the position. Having some knowledge of what was happening and possessing a private pilot's license myself, I could pretty well make out the whole picture. Every time our planes would dive on the position there would be ground fire returned.

There is nothing more deadly to an airplane than being in range of small arms fire. After four passes or so, they were ready to unload the napalm and were circling in a left-hand pattern away from the target and heading our direction to give themselves room to line up on target. I believe the target and objective at that time would have been northeast of our position.

Suddenly, over the radio, we heard someone tell one of the pilots that he was smoking. In a very excited voice, he asked, "Whose lines are we over?" He was told everything was okay; he was over our lines. The other pilot said he'd take a closer look at the smoking plane.

He pulled up under and said, "Yeah, you have smoke." About that time, the planes were at an altitude of about 1500 feet and the smoke became visible to us on the ground.

The pilot of the smoking plane said, "Everything is reading okay. I'll try to make it.

Stick with me."

"Roger."

By then, the plane was directly over our area. Suddenly, black smoke and orange fire burst from the engine.

"It's getting hot! I'm getting out!" the very excited voice cried. In an excellent display of airmanship, he rolled inverted with canopy open, pushed the nose up with his foot and the negative Gs popped him out of the plane. He cleared the tail and popped the chute. Everyone in the battalion was cheering, and no doubt he could hear it. I was cheering and watching that pilotless, black, smoking airplane turn nose down in a Split S and knew that the speed of the plane would pull the nose up. I shouted to watch that plane.

"It's going into a Split S!"

Then there was complete silence as the plane came rushing in our direction at about 300 kt. You could feel the helplessness of the moment, everyone looking in every direction for a place to hide. Fortunately, the nose did not come up horizontally, but the plane crashed and exploded in a very spectacular manner—just short of our area.

The dark came; the rain came. We crossed the river which was knee deep and started up the ridges of Kanmabong and, unknown to us at the time, up Hill 749. Artillery constantly passed over our heads, their mortars searching us out. We had one new kid that hit the deck so often I think he put on the equivalent of ten miles up and down, up and down.

We came to a spot where there was a large tree that was lying across the path, and we were told it was booby trapped and to not put our weight on the tree. The paths by now were like grease, extremely difficult to make uphill headway. We were wet and muddy. The engineers were there helping each individual over the tree. The column was halted at one point while elements of the Seventh Regiment came down the path. We stood off to the side while they passed. There was the usual "Anybody here named ———?" Sometimes the person was there and there would be a brief exchange of greetings. Olson and I were standing next to each other as one of the Seventh Regiment members was being helped over the tree.

Someone behind this individual said, "Mr. LeBaron…" I don't remember what the statement was, but the person being helped over the tree responded.

It was like a magnet grabbing something toward it. Olson, the football semi-pro, immediately pounced on the situation and rushed forward, shouting, "Are you Eddie LeBaron? Are you Eddie LeBaron?" Grabbing him by the arm, shaking his hand, he repeated, "Are you Eddie LeBaron?" as they both fell back against the downed tree. The engineers, LeBaron, me and everyone nearby didn't know what to think.

Then LeBaron was saying, "Yes, yes!"

Olson was bearing down on him and the engineers were screaming, "What the hell are you doing? Are you crazy? Get back there; you'll kill us all!"

With a lot of cussing by the engineers and to the bewilderment of LeBaron, who was not a large man, Olson stepped back unperturbed by the commotion he caused by his friendly assault on LeBaron and kept repeating, "That's Eddie LeBaron! That's Eddie LeBaron!" The Seventh continued happily sliding down the muddy path into reserve.

The morning of September 13, I woke up in the foxhole. I had a replacement with me. About 0700, I was sitting up and heard, "Hallo, Hallo." It was sort of the way the British say *hello*. At first, I saw no one when I looked around, but once again I heard the greeting. I saw a hand waving and the top of a head over the edge of the hole, sort of a "Kilroy" style. I was baffled at first, thought perhaps some Brit soldier had made it back to our lines overnight.

I said, "Hello, who are you?" The hand waved again. This time, it had some whitish paper in it. I then shouted, "Etewa! Etewa!" taking the safety off my rifle. He stuck his head up and it was clearly a North Korean. He nodded, smiled, and waved his hand, held up a sneaker, and then bent down again. I shouted to Joe, "We have something here."

Joe ran up with BAR, leveled it, and also shouted, "Etewa! Etewa!" Finally out of the hole came a North Korean officer grinning, with his dirty hands up, saying, "Hallo, hallo," bowing every few steps. I realized he was probably no threat as he must have sneaked into that hole sometime during the night unarmed. He made it clear he wanted to surrender and asked for a "butt," gesturing with two fingers to his mouth, obviously looking for a cigarette. We notified the lieutenant. He came up with an interpreter and suggested we search the area for more.

There had been two or three sharp firefights about that time in the area of Easy Company. They lasted only minutes each but were to go on all day and night. Our unit didn't get hit until about 1400 hours. Shortly after hearing the firing and mortars, I found a helmet lying on the ground. There were many, and I decided I'd better try to get accustomed to it. We were dug in along the ridgeline that overlooked a couple hundred yards of tall grass. The unit in front of us, separated by a valley or small ravine, was coming under fire. There was a lot of commotion with gunners and assistants running up to take some pressure off. Then we started receiving mortars so suddenly that it was startling! The higher ground past us and the other unit was, it turns out, Hill 749. Out of the deep grass area, the North Koreans opened up with machine guns. They started raking us and there were no holes to get into. The lead was really flying, mortars crunching down, many people hit.

Right in front of me was about a twelve-foot high dead pine tree with a branch about ten inches thick sticking out on each side. I was able to stand up and could see over the tall grass. I watched the grass bend over from the muzzle blast when they fired. About that time a machine gunner and assistant came along the path, crouched down, looking for a place to get some cover and set up their gun. I motioned to them to where a place had been leveled out behind and to the right of where I stood. They scooted in there and were setting up their gun. I then concentrated on the enemy, got a good look at where the grass was disturbed when they fired. I aimed for where I guessed they should be and fired eight quick rounds there. I must have done some damage because, in seconds, I had several rounds whistle by me. I ducked down just in time to see two rounds go completely through the tree I was behind, turning around in time to see one of the machine gunners shot in the head.

The firing on us stopped as fast as it started, but they were shouting for us to get up on the other ridge. We had to run down this path, through a little valley that was cobwebbed with communications wire. I was still wearing the helmet I found when Joe yelled, "Let's go!" He struck out on the run, firing to his left from the hip. I followed behind. With my stupid damn luck and that damn helmet, one of the straps on the helmet caught or hooked a damn wire, jerking my head around to the left, and I stopped short right in the open. In my haste (and my swearing at that frigging helmet), I could hear everyone shouting, "Come on! Come on!" The bullets were zinging around and while pulling as hard as my neck and body could against the force of that wire, I finally reached behind the helmet and flipped it off my head vowing never again to don one of those piss pots. The tension on the wire caused the helmet to spring away and it did a loop and came back and hit me in the jaw.

When I finally made it up the other side, they told me I was just like a cow's tail that's always on the end and covered with shit. They also told me the only reason I didn't get shot was because their gunners were laughing so hard they couldn't shoot straight. I was dragging communication wire, grass, branches, and who knows what else.

Shortly after that, our other corpsman May was hit. Joe and I helped carry him out. Contrareas took over the duties of corpsman. Contrareas was a very brave person.

There were sounds of voices, whistles, sharp orders shouted, and an officer urging on a team that was struggling to get a heavy machine gun up to the ridge. I could distinctly hear a squeaking sound like dry metal against metal. This officer gave an exceptionally loud, sharp command, and I couldn't resist shouting, "Hey, Wambu, get some grease you rickshaw-pulling Wambu!" That apparently was ignored, but he issued another sharp order, and I shouted again, "F— you!" This he definitely understood and I believe he shouted back something about doing the same for Harry Truman and John Foster Dulles. I looked at Joe and wondered, *Who?* Just as someone yelled to knock it off, Joe also warned me to keep it down. I guess I was just talking tough because I felt pretty tense. Wambu means turtle in Chinese, and it was very insulting to call someone a turtle.

The next day was fair weather with shooting taking place in several directions, and we were still following the ridgeline upward when, while resting, I heard the trickle of water nearby. A few feet into the brush I discovered a beautiful, tiny stream of clear, cool water. I emptied my canteens and filled them with the fresh water. Others followed until an officer saw us all huddled and told us to get back on the path. I felt quite smug because I had cheated a little and gotten away with this ever so precious water, until about fifty yards up the path was a small area where the water formed a pond and lying in the pond were three dead, bloated North Koreans. All I could do was add Halazone tabs and hope I could find a water point before I became really thirsty.

I am not sure of the order in which some of the following took place. I was told of Gomez on September 14 but cannot remember clearly how the 13th and 14th went by. On the morning of the 14th, I was standing on a mound digging a hole (seems like I was always digging a hole) when Contrareas, who was the company runner, said, "Conway," with his Mexican accent.

"Yeah, Contrareas," I answered. "You knew Lefty Gomez?"

"You mean Ed Gomez?"

"Ya, Ed."

'Why?"

"Well, the cops in Omaha will be glad to hear he is dead."

"When did Ed get it?"

"Oh, this morning. You heard the shooting."

"Why will the cops be glad?"

"Well, he was a sort of a desperado." Contrareas then came up the mound, taking out of his jacket pocket a crumpled envelope and said, "Here, read this." It was a letter to Ed's mother and sister telling them to not feel bad if he was killed as he would have died for his country and hoping he would be decorated for bravery so his dad could be proud of him.

I teared up a little bit and could not help thinking about Eddie for a few seconds, remembering him saying, "I hope they don't run out of medals before I get there." I asked Contrareas how he was killed. He didn't know; he was in the CP when Easy Company called in their casualty report. I thought to myself, *Well Eddie, you didn't make it.* But he did indeed. I learned some months later that he was awarded the Medal of Honor.

Ed had smothered a hand grenade with his body to save his crew. I also learned later that he had been in a reformatory as an early teen. It was called the Omaha Industrial School for Boys, not far from the famous Father Flannagan Orphanage at Boys Town.

So back to the war, we were so fortunate to be involved in. According to Chesty, Reg. Commander Puller, most people have to wait twenty years between wars; we only had to wait five. On September 15, we were just lounging alongside the path when the colonel came by saying, "You men, go down the ridge line and pick up all the ammo and stretchers you can carry and bring it up." About ten to twelve of us went and began picking up rifles, helmets, ammo, grenades, and stretchers and placed them along the path. On the way back we would carry as much as we could.

Suddenly, just as everything takes place in a combat area, a land mine! You can tell a mine by the geyser of dirt it shoots up into the air. I heard shouting, "I'm hit, I'm hit!"

"Stay where you're at!"

"Help me, I'm bleeding! My foot is gone!"

"Stay still!" As I headed down there was another blast, another geyser, more screaming. Then I got to the spot where the mines went off. There were four people, sitting, holding their legs, holding their bodies, with another soldier on the path in shock.

One of them was Hoover, our corpsman, and one of the others was McGee. I don't remember the names of the other two. Also lying there was a North Korean who, at first, I thought was dead. There was no one else around that I could see except for a couple people on a rise about fifty yards away uphill, lying pressed against the side of the hill. They could move because I saw them walking seconds before. Two of the injured each had one foot half taken off. Hoover was hit in the legs and arm but would be able to move except that he was afraid to. The fourth was hit in the bladder with one small but very painful wound. I shouted to the group lying on the hillside to come down and give me a hand. They stood up, started walking toward me, and stopped, shaking their heads and pointing at the ground in front of them. I told them to go out to the path as I knew that was free of mines as I had been there myself shortly before. They refused to come down, which really got me pissed. I took the carbine from the guy sitting on the path and fired a round about ten feet from that bunch. That was the last time I saw them. They practically jumped over the crest of the hill.

Trying to assure the injured guys that I could get them out, I started in toward them, digging my feet deep into the soil so I could follow them out and step in the same places. I encountered one mine near the path I was taking, and pretending this was old stuff, I laid on the ground, stuck my bayonet under the cover, closed my eyes, hid my face, and told the others (over their protests) to do the same. Then I flipped the cover off like an old pro.

Finally, I got up to the first guy. Fortunately, he was not a large man; neither was the second guy. I had been a weight lifter of sorts most of my life, so lifting 130 pounds wasn't much of a challenge. I lifted McGee up, although he was very apprehensive, and assured him I could hold him and still see my footmarks okay. I carried him to the path and that seemed to be of some reassurance to the others. I picked up the second guy, told Hoover to come behind and step only in my footprints. He did, and we got out. Then I looked back at the North Korean and when I looked he closed his eyes like he expected me to maybe shoot him. I went back in and picked him up. He was really a lot lighter than I expected, and I almost threw him up in the air. He was covered with dirt and smelled terrible.

I then went up the path, Hoover behind me, telling me how great I was and that he now thought the Marine Corps was the greatest—180 degrees from what he thought prior to that. I notified a sergeant that we had wounded and needed to gather them up, and so it happened, they were helicoptered out. I saw all of them a few weeks later in the hospital in Yohosuka. Two of them had a leg amputated.

CHAPTER 6

On September 15, we relieved Easy Company and were told we would go into the attack late in the afternoon after an air strike and artillery barrage were to take place. We would move out when we saw two rounds of white phosphorous go off. Why were we waiting until 1700? I thought it must be pretty well finished and we would take the hill just before dark. Third Platoon had the point, and as usual, Joe and I found it difficult to wait all day. So the two of us, along with Pete Cusik (who was a very reluctant participant), started working our way up to the point. To our right was a horseshoe shape in the terrain and unbeknownst to anyone, there was a honeycomb of bunkers, all designed to protect the bunker at the very tip of Hill 749. They were lying there quietly. We were not far from the point. An 18-year-old kid—blond, with blue eyes—came up to me, squatted down, looked at me in a manner that I could detect his anxiety, and said to me, "I have the point. Is this it?"

I replied, "I guess so."

"Do you think it will be tough?"

I lied and told him, "We've been hitting them for four days. They're nervous. They won't have good aim." Or something like that. I almost told him I would take the point for him, but hesitated.

The air strike came on, and so did many mortars from the North Koreans. The artillery laid in a heavy concentration. Then came the two white phosphorous the military called "Willy Peter".

"OK, get the point moving." The blond kid looked at me, hesitated. I told him, "Let's go meet the tiger."

We started out. One squad went to the left of the path, and there were some troops on the right. Two shots sounded and the kid went down, shot through the heart. When he hit the ground, his head was turned and he was looking at me with his helmet pushed up, lying on the left side of his head and face. I thought at first he was alive but could then see that fixed stare and his pale, blue eyes. I felt guilty as though I could have said something that would have maybe prevented him from getting killed.

Joe said, "Let's go!" I had been pretty cavalier about things prior to that, but I admit the incident shook me some.

You don't have time really to think about things under those circumstances, and by now there was firing all along the line. Cusik was saying to Joe, "We don't have to be here. I don't like this. Let's wait here. Joe, this isn't our platoon." We were on the ground and could see ahead of us this large bunker on the very tip of the ridgeline, looking very threatening with flashes from the muzzles of at least two machine guns spraying the area.

The unit on our left was against real stiff resistance. We were in the center, pinned down. The unit on the right seemed to be moving ahead, when those bunkers in the horseshoe-shaped crevice suddenly opened up on them, really slicing into them. At the same time, the left flank was hit by an attack that materialized in the wooded area. They were stunned and began to fall back. Where we were, we could see over their heads. The North Koreans were coming at them in the brush. In spite of the fire from the bunker trying to keep us down, we were able to deliver fire effectively enough to stop them. Then, as though we knew what the other was thinking, we got up and ran forward, firing where we last saw them in that brush. Our "charge" cooled the action down, at least long enough so the Third Platoon could get another foothold there. The mortars were coming in sporadically, so no one could move ahead very well because every place seemed covered.

Joe started creeping on his belly with some trees blocking the view of the gunners in the bunker and fire from the cover hindered by the height of the ridgeline. I started after him. We were able to get in position undetected and took deliberate aim at the opening of the bunker. We could faintly see movement behind the guns. I waited until Joe fired the BAR, then I fired when he was loading. In this way we temporarily neutralized this bunker. By now the others were coming up behind and delivering fire, so Joe and I were able to get closer. By now the Second Platoon was coming up in the open. Joe and I talked about rushing the bunker, but I was very apprehensive on that at this time, stating that we would have to contend with mines and also with the fire from the caves, which we could now see were designed to cover this area. The men on our right were trying to deal with the caves and bunkers on the wall of the crevice. They were trying flamethrowers, lowering explosives and throwing grenades to keep them down.

Suddenly I noticed explosions, small explosions, all around us. For a few seconds I was really baffled until a low roar above us told us the FO had called in an air strike. Normally an air strike, especially by the Marine Corsairs, was a welcome sight, but in this case we were the recipients of their power show. Shortly, there were more explosions and another roar. A large, black F4U (U-bird) went over. Now we were just hoping the North Koreans in the bunker would not take advantage of this and drill our asses.

Guys were shouting to get the air panels out and get those planes on target. One guy stood out in the open waving an air panel when down he went—hit or not, I do not know. We were lying as flat as we could, one of the most helpless feelings ever.

Nowhere to hide, and our planes still had their bombs and napalm! Everyone knew what napalm would do if dropped, so after a couple more guys courageously stood up waving air panels that were ignored, Joe made a very bold, last-ditch effort raising his BAR, yelling, "Who's side are you on, you son of a bitch?" With that, he fired a short burst that you could see like powder kick up on impact on the right wing. The plane veered left.

No smoke occurred and the plane got back into the pattern, circling once again. By then, the air FO must have gotten the message to them, for they seemed to look the place over once more. In they came again, but this time their fire was on target into the caves and bunkers on the wall of the crevice, where they dropped their bombs and the napalm with very positive effect. How we truly loved those guys.

With no time to comment, we turned our attention back to the bunker and decided we needed more grenades. We shouted back for grenades, which were thrown up to us in an ammo bandolier. They landed at the foot of a tree several yards short of us. A hand reached out from behind the tree, picked up the bandolier, and threw it forward, still short of our position. I got a look at the owner of that well-placed hand. It was Weaver, the leader of the Rebels, who must have been confused about where the front was. I slid down to grasp the grenades and couldn't restrain myself from shouting, "Hey, Weaver!" He looked around the tree with his big, round eyes, and I continued, 'Where are your Rebels now?" He just blinked and went back behind the tree.

Then I saw Lieutenant Bernie Adams who had been shot in the upper right thigh and was leaning back against a stretcher that was being held up on one end by two guys while a corpsman was trying to treat the wound by cutting away the trouser leg. I didn't know him by name but had seen him many times. He was the platoon leader of the Second Platoon. At this time, he was talking on the field phone with a sergeant standing near him looking quite apprehensive, probably because he did not dare duck if his wounded lieutenant was standing.

I got the grenades up to Joe, but we were both keeping an eye on the bunker and at the same time watching the lieutenant. It just looked so out of place, and I thought to myself, why the hell doesn't John Wayne there give the platoon to the sergeant and get the hell under some cover? Suddenly the lieutenant started waving his arms and shouting, "Get back, get back! They're coming around behind us! Get back! Pull back!"

I didn't know what to make of that. All the guys I could see were facing toward our direction or to the right. Then I thought maybe I couldn't see over the ridge near the caves; maybe they're hitting us there. I figured, shit, we just about had this place. Now we'll have to do it again. It was almost twilight now. I don't remember Joe's reaction to this setback.

Everyone started back, walking backward and firing from the hip at no real target to hold the enemies' heads down. We backed right across the right side of our column, back from the caves, through a field of tall grass. As far as I could tell we were not fired on at all during this maneuver. While sitting in this tall grass, trying to not give any snipers a crack at myself, everyone was confused. There were no signs of any counterattack. It looked as though it was deserted where we just left. Soon Captain Hale was going among the men asking what happened: why the pullback. He looked at me and asked directly, "Why did you pull back?"

Observing the very painful look on his face, a look of anguish, I answered, "The lieutenant ordered everyone to pull back, Captain."

He went on, still asking, "Why, why?" We pulled back to the positions we were in the night before. There was a lot of confusion.

CHAPTER 7

(Just a note here to tell you of a young kid I had in the hole with me. When we dug the hole the night of the fourteenth, there were several dead North Koreans we had to dig in amongst. After dragging a couple away from the place we decided to dig, there were two lying only a few feet in front of the hole. I told the kid, "Shovel some dirt onto their faces so they won't be looking at us all night."

He took a scoop of dirt, held it over the first body, but could not convince himself to drop it on the body, stating, "His eyes are open."

I answered him, "That's okay, he won't feel it."

He hesitated again, remarking, "His mouth is open too." I finally let him dig our hole and took care of the dead bodies myself.)

Before we could get settled in, word came down to have Joe Vittori and a rifleman go up to the point with Second Platoon. I shouted to Weaver, who was fifty yards or so away, and told him what the word was. He stopped, looked down with a very tired, painful look. Everyone was waiting for his order, so I finally said, "Oh hell, I'll go."

I was packing my gear, stuffing grenades in my pockets, and told Joe to wait a minute, but he didn't. I started down the path and a guy held up a Thompson machine gun, telling me to take it if it would help. I scooped it up with my left arm, forgetting how awkward and heavy they were. It immediately started hitting me in the knee with every step. I almost shit-canned it.

When I finally trudged to the hole we were to share, Joe was making it somewhat larger. I began making a ledge on the left side and in front under the front edge, a place to put our grenades. Joe was laying his magazines on the edge of the hole. There were several grenades there when I arrived plus the six or so I brought, but I did not hesitate to send word back to our platoon sergeant Kester to bring a case of grenades up to Conaway on the point.

A sergeant or corporal, an Italian chap I had seen in Joe's company on other occasions, came up assigning positions to some Second Platoon members. Seeing Joe, he asked, "Hey, Vittori, what the hell you doing up here?"

Joe answered, "Second Platoon always needs help."

"Oh shit, you're looking for a Purple Heart!"

"Already have one," came Joe's reply.

"Oh, then you want the Congress, huh?" he said jokingly as he moved. (In reference to the Congressional Medal of Honor.)

Joe did not answer, but about a minute later, we were still busying ourselves when he said, "Ya, I'd like the Congress, but I don't want to die for it." I grunted in agreement and the subject was dropped.

Shortly after that, Kester came up with a case of grenades on his shoulder, walked right past about ten yards away from us headed into North Korean country, so I yelled, "Kester!

Where are you going?"

He answered, "Bringing these grenades to the point."

"This is it!" I called to him.

"Oh, oh, oh!" was his reply as he came sprinting back into our lines.

Well, the stage was set. The next move was theirs. I would guess the time to be around 2200 hours. I did not realize then how our position would impact us. If they would have been further uphill they would not have been so easily overrun. There was no time—it was getting dark. There were too many at once. There were seven holes to our right and front which we had to constantly remember so we would not fire into them. Later I would realize how horseshit the setup was. If those guys in front would have been up the hill another ten yards or so, they would have fared much better. Guess there was no time to move them, and hindsight is always much clearer.

In front of the seven machine gun positions was a clear area about the size of a tennis court. Beyond that was brush and what appeared to be a drop-off. From what I remember about that afternoon, we were in the same area where Joe and I fired so effectively into them on our earlier foray. To the front were those bushes, like willows with several tall jack pine trees spread around. Further to the right was that menacing-looking bunker. We could not see beyond the brush, but we knew that's where the heavies were set up, covering the ridgeline to the bunkers. Two of the tall jack pines were close to us, just to our right.

The artillery field officer was up the hill, over the crest, and about 2230 hours or so, he passed the word for everyone to hunker down in their holes. He was going to lay some fire down right in front. We did, and he did what I would call a spectacular job, which made me a little more comfortable feeling that we would have that fire when we needed it.

About 2300 hours, we were hearing a lot of voices, whistles and other noises out front. When we could see movements from time to time we would throw grenades. Some of these movements, I now know, were meant for us to see so we would not notice the infiltrators crawling up under our positions. It was very dark when the moon was hidden and very bright when the moon shone down, producing an eerie feeling. One of their tricks was to slowly pull a tree branch down so that it would not be noticed, and then suddenly let it spring back up. That drew a grenade every time.

We were straining to see and hear anything possible when, again, there was a flash on a mountain top about a mile or so out. Joe and I looked at each other and ducked. Sure enough, it was a 76 and you could hear that sucker wind up two seconds before it hit. With a sharp crack it detonated in the top of the pine trees, shrapnel whizzing and buzzing all over. Again and again one of the guys was shouting in a very frightened manner, "Kenny! Kenny! Kenny's dead! Kenny's dead!"

Someone else shouted back, "Shut up! Straighten up!" After several rounds, an SNJ-Advanced Navy trainer used as a spotter plane came over, and I got a glimpse of it in the moonlight. The 76 was silenced, but many other sounds emerged from the hills of Korea, and it wasn't hatchet bird! How I wished for a helmet now!

All of us were short of sleep. I suggested we try to get some sleep, saying I would take first watch. Joe curled up in the left corner, and I got behind the BAR. After a few minutes, Joe sat up and said, "I can't sleep. You try." And sleep I did. I was sound asleep when Joe shook me and warned, "Here they come! Here they come!" And a heavy machine gun opened up spraying the area. I could not see clearly, I was so sleepy. Joe kept saying, "Look at 'em, look at 'em!" and everything broke at once like a crash.

Joe was firing steadily, and finally I could at least see the muzzle blasts. They were everywhere, but we had to remember the guys in front of us. The noise was deafening. The firing was so heavy that I think it helped light up the place. I saw two or three figures crawling up the slope. They crawled between two of our gun positions and behind all of them. I fired into them but had to remember our gunners. After firing about ten clips, I grabbed the next clip, inserted it, and my rifle jammed. The damn clip had a long round in it, even though I tamped them all down earlier. I could not close the bolt. I could not open it either. Joe was firing furiously. I was hitting my gun with my fist, not able to think of anything else to use. Never occurred I could have used my foot. I had thought of asking Joe to hit it with the butt of his BAR, but he was too busy. I was going to use a grenade, but just as I struck the handle with the grenade, there was a blinding flash. And I was struck in the head and face. I instinctively yelled, and as I grabbed my face, I got hit again in the shoulder and fell down into the corner of the hole. I was stunned and trying to figure things out. I don't know if I was briefly unconscious, but I was sure scrambled. Joe was still firing, inches from my head at one point, and my ears were aching. Then the real shocker. I was blind! I couldn't see! I looked up toward Joe but could only see faint flashes of light and that scared me more than I could have possibly imagined.

As my eyes filled with tears, I asked that if there is a God, please help me now. What would I do if they overran us? I felt helpless. The tears washed the blood out of my eyes, and I could at least see with my right eye. My left eye and head were too swollen to allow any sight. I don't know how long I was feeling sorry for myself but finally realized how frantically Joe was still firing and knew I'd better contribute something. I got up on my knees, still feeling unsure. Joe, seeing I was moving, quickly looked over at me and said, "You're hit bad," and then shouted for a corpsman. He immediately went back to firing the BAR. I could hardly hear him, so I was sure no one else had either. I would never have expected anyone to try getting to our position anyway. When I looked up the slope, the fifteen feet or so to the crest, I could see bullets hitting the ground so closely it looked like it was being swept by a broom. When I was looking out front and feeling around for my rifle, which I couldn't find, I noticed several little grass fires scattered around and could see the muzzles on the machine guns were red hot.

About that time, I believe Joe was hit. I heard a hit, saw Joe jerk, look down, stop firing, and rub his chest. I said nothing. He looked at me and said, "Where the hell are they getting their ammo?" Then in slow motion, as though he were adjusting something on a table, he picked up his BAR and commenced firing again.

I started lobbing grenades where I saw muzzle flashes or movement in the brushy area. I pulled the pins with my right hand—blood running down my arm—threw with my left hand. I tried plugging the holes with my fingers but realized that I had to contribute any way I could. It's surprising how well a person can do as a lefty when they're scared.

Our machine guns were getting knocked out one at a time. It was difficult to protect them with grenades. Joe alternated firing to the left, then the right, then down the center. I did my best to lob grenades beyond our holes. The gun closest to us was operated by a big, husky guy. A grenade from the bushes exploded in or near his hole. He leaned over the top of his gun, the barrel red hot, still firing when another grenade exploded. He fell over the gun and it appeared his hair caught fire. Where the hell were they getting all their ammo? The longer the fight went on the more intense it became.

They must have been rushing in troops as soon as the others were hit or out of ammo.

Joe asked me to "load some magazines, but don't load them backwards like Pete does." I had to take M-1 clips, pull the cartridges out of them and load them into the magazines, a tricky job when you have two hands functioning properly. Out of the eight rounds in a clip, I was lucky to get three or four rounds into the magazine. Bullets were scattered all around the bottom of the hole and we were running low on ammo.

With the light from the many small fires burning, I noticed there were several bodies in front of our position, hopefully all dead. Joe must have got them, and I hoped one of them was the grenade thrower who got me. Of course I had thrown much of my own case and a half of grenades, which would be totally gone before the end of the action.

All the machine gun barrels were red hot, firing as fast as they could load the belts. One after another there would be an orange-red flash and another gun knocked out, and North Koreans swarming them. Now I had to throw grenades and try to bracket the holes.

Some of the magazines I handed Joe had only three or four rounds in them. I had thrown all my grenades. The North Koreans were running back and forth, seemingly in confusion, with whistles and shouting, silhouetted by the small fires. I sure wished I had a 12-gauge shotgun right then.

I started scrambling around the bottom of the hole looking for more grenades when I grabbed the stock of the Thompson gun. I had completely forgotten about it. I pulled it out from under my sleeping bag, which was covered with dirt and gravel. The single magazine I had for it was in the gun. I also had the two grenades in my dungaree jacket pockets. I now had something to lash out with, but I did not need to put the gun to my shoulder. Through some special blessing the firing just ceased. When the firing stopped, I thought at first I had gone stone deaf. Joe was just staring out at the commotion with the North Koreans, dozens of them lying dead or rolling around trying to get up, moaning, shouting every now and then. There had been so much smoke and cordite in the air earlier that it was difficult to breathe and see at times. Now that the air was clearing, it looked spooky, but at least no one was paying any attention to us. It was like we weren't there.

Without saying anything, Joe slid out of the hole with his BAR, went down to where the gun was knocked out with the gunner lying on top of it. He pulled the gunner off, grabbed the machine gun, trying to lift the cover to pull the belt out. Out of the wooded area, slightly to Joe's right, came several North Koreans who stood there, looking and gesturing at the hillside. My heart was in my throat. Joe tugged on the belt and the gun fell into the hole. The North Koreans sure noticed that. Joe stopped and laid back on his side. I was struggling with myself, my head spinning. Does my gun fire? Would a grenade get Joe too? Is Joe in my line of fire? Does Joe have any ammo left? The North Koreans moved forward a few feet, still bunched up. Joe turned and let go with a burst, hitting them good. They dropped and scattered, firing wildly, unable to see Joe or me. I had a clear shot now. The Thompson worked, as I let go about ten rounds. I got one short burst in return. I didn't think of it at the time, but they sure must have wondered where we came from.

Joe scurried back to the hole and I threw one of my two remaining grenades. We were covered with dirt, and I believe Joe was bleeding. But he said nothing about it.

Instead, he looked at me and said, "We have to get help up here. We're out of ammo, you're hit bad. You get up the hill, and I'll cover you." He crawled out of the hole again as I stood up. It was the first time I tried to stand. I was really weak, so when I put my foot on the edge of the hole to give myself a push, my leg just quivered.

I went down again on my knees, and Joe said again, "Go ahead, I'll cover you!" And those were his last words.

Joe was squatting, turned slightly, and there was a crack—a zit sound and a splat. Joe screamed, grabbed his face, and fell over. I shouted, "Joe! Joe!" He was lying with his head down the hill and his feet near the edge of the hole. As I grabbed his foot I felt him quiver and moan—just once, and that was it. Damn, so close to making it. I threw my last grenade and fired what I had left in the magazine. With great effort, I made it up over the edge and fell into a hole where someone, I believe the FO, put a .45 in my face. His eyes were like saucers. I bet mine were too. I gasped, "Marine, wounded!" They immediately moved to help me.

I asked who was in charge. They pointed left, said "Lieutenant," and I made my way down the path a few yards, asking for the lieutenant but got no answer. I said *lieutenant* once again and a voice answered, "Watch who you're calling *lieutenant!*" I said I was sorry and told him where our position was, suggesting he get two BARs in there by having the guys slide down on their bellies and set up a couple of machine guns on the edge of the drop off. I then asked them to double check on Joe, although I knew he was dead. He asked me if I needed help. I asked him if the path I was on led to battalion aide. When he said it was, I told him I could make it.

When I got back to the aide station, there were dozens of wounded and dead lying there under the trees. Just after I got there and they gave me a stretcher to lie on, mortar shells and 76 came in on us. I told the doctor that I was leaving, going down the path where maybe it would be safer. He tried to talk me into waiting until daylight, but I said, "I made it this far. I'm not going to get it lying on a stretcher." I remembered that path all too well anyway.

Once I made it to the river, though, I did not know where to go from there. I sat down beside the burning ruins of a Korean hut, wondering if I would bleed to death before I figured out where I was. I was afraid to go to the river to drink even though I was the thirstiest I had ever been. Then, out in the dark, I heard some talking, and someone moaning in pain. North Koreans? I didn't know until I heard some scrambling like someone fell, heard more moans, and then heard someone say, "Son of a bitch!"

Those were the sweetest cuss words I ever heard and, like an idiot, I went running in their direction, yelling, "Hey, guys!" just as the one guy with a rifle took aim. Luckily, he didn't shoot. There were five men carrying one on a stretcher. They were all wounded, with the guy on the stretcher hit in the jaw. All he could do was make pained, unintelligible sounds as he tried to keep from choking.

We talked about where we were. No one knew for sure, but we agreed we would have to cross the river to the road on the other side. This was the road we had come up from our reserve area, but how far away was help? When we got to the river's edge, I saw what kind of water it was, but I could not help myself. I drank from the river.

Once on the road, I suggested everyone wait where we were, while I took the carbine (I really felt naked without a weapon) and walked up the road. The road went up grade for about a hundred yards, seventy-five to one hundred feet above the river. Once at the top, I witnessed another beautiful sight. There were trucks with lights on moving around a perimeter of guns. They had lights in the tents, people moving all around.

I shouted back to the wounded group, "Come on, we don't have far to go."

When our rag-tag band emerged from the dark, wounded and haggard, the encampment was astonished. Everyone poured out to help. They treated us like royalty and called in some ambulances. I was put into an ambulance along with the chap who was hit in the jaw, and as we were moving down behind a row of 155s, one of them fired. I saw it fire, so I knew what it was. But the other guy thought it was incoming. I assured him it was okay. That was the last gun I ever heard fired in anger. I was finished. Once I lay back, I never got back on my feet again except to relieve myself and to prove to the doctors that I could still move, though very weak.

It gave me a lot of time to think of how fortunate I was to be alive, how it all came about, that long, rugged path that brought me to where I was, and the brave men I met along the way. Mostly I remembered the most special friend Joe Vittori, and I was overcome with grief.

Lyle Conaway, Cpl., USMCR
Fox Co, Second Battalion, First Regiment, First Marine Division
Third Platoon, Third Squad
March–September 1951
Respectfully transcribed by
Mary Lou Conaway, daughter-in-law

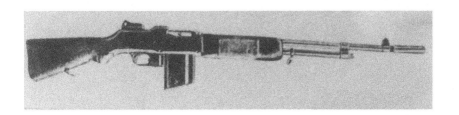

BAR SONG

(In reference to the Browning Automatic Riffle)
BLESS 'EM ALL

This weapon I carry, she weighs half a ton;
The damn thing is 40 feet long,
I fire it in hundreds
While others by one.
Hark goes the poor bar man's song.

Bless 'em all, Bless 'em all
The A.P., the tracer, the ball;
Pull back the change lever,
Pull back on the bolt
Squeeze on the trigger and wait for the jolt.
Oh she kicks like a Model T Ford
And death is your only reward
We know when we're dead
Some other shithead
Will pick up the BAR we adore.

The following are hand-written notes I would like to share of my life, my time in the service and flight escapades on the Iron Range in Minnesota.

Kyle Conaway

Born, May 8, 1930. Virginia Mn. family then resided at 1908 Wolford, Ridgewood add. Parents were Cecil & Ruth. I was 5th of 3 girls 3 boys, which eventually totaled 8 children. We lived at this add. until 1938, when our house burned and we moved to a place called the Martin Farm, half way between Mt Iron and Parkville. 1938 was also the year I remember a local pilot named Bud Hill. was flying during the night and was blinded by the lights of auto that surrounded the airport, causing Hill to crash his airplane into his new Ford auto he had parked with lights on, on the field to use as a reference point. I remember well the airshows that were put on at the old airport, the old Tri motor airplanes, the auto-gyro; the sky writers who always spelled out "Phillips 66" with the smoke. I was always fascinated by the planes.

We lived in the Mt Iron area for a few years and moved back to Va. in the Finntown area on 2nd st No. a dumpy house. I will always remember that era because it was where I lived when the Japanese attacked Pearl Harbor.

We then moved to Wms add, all the kids 17 and older were enlisting in the service. My older brother Larry joined the Marines in '43. was wounded in the 1st wave to hit the beach of Saipan. Many of the guys were killed, Muriel Ring, Fuzzy Somma, Mecky Orieman Coombs. My cousin Virgil Conaway, a dive bomber pilot aboard the U.S.S. Hancock. - many more.

I attended Va. Jr. High, I was a wise guy, one that should have had his butt kicked about every week, (sometimes I did) I thought I knew it all. I quit school when I lied my age to join the Marine Corps.

I enlisted U.S.M.C. Dec. 1945, tho I did not leave immediatly I was very important that to get enlisted by a certain date to qualify as a W W II status, to obtain the benefits of the G.I. bill and also to take advantage of an aviation duty only contract.

In 1946 I served aboard the U.S.S. Shangri-La C.V. for a short period of time. Was there transfered to Ewa air field, Oahu Hawaii, where I was given a short course in operation

53

of the .50 cal machine gun, safty technique around aircraft, use of parachutes, fire fighting equip. ~~ect~~ emergency tactics ect.

Was then assigned to ~~VMR 153~~ VMR 153, served in asiatic pacific theater for awhile, traveled to Islands of, Johnston, Kwajalein, Midway, Guam. Went to Tsingtao China and was assigned to a fighter unit, VMF 115, I then travelled to Teentsin, where I stayed in the French arsenal for a few wks and then on to Peiping, Nanyuan airfield, which was also called, South Feild. This sqdrn was formerly comanded by Col Joe Foss, who shot down 26 jap planes, ~~served~~ as gov. of So. Dak.

While In China, our units, especially our line companies were caught in between the battles waged between the Chinese Nationalists and the Route army of Ma Tse Tung. Our units lost several planes to ground fire and sabotage during these times, and there were several men killed ~~and~~ wounded and captured during these skirmishes.

At one point during my China tour, I was assigned to guard duty aboard a train that took us to the sea port of Taku, where I remember seeing, many hundreds of cases of amunition and Thompson Sub machine guns piled on the docks, unloaded from ships. Little did I know at that time what those guns were going to mean to me in the future.

In the spring of '47 the U.S. was forced out of China by the Communists, I went back to Guam, and there back to Ewa Feild in Hawaii.

I was discharged in ~~the~~ June of '47 from the Great Lakes Naval Trng center. As I was 17 yrs of age at discharge, I had deficulty finding ~~work~~ employment until I reached 18 yrs. I took up flying on the G.I. Bill at the Va. airport, with a flying school called Northeast Airways, this school was run by Ray Glumak and Art Tomes, It was an excellent school and provided a variety of light aircraft, including some surplus military trainers. Single eng. land and float, even a twin cessna, UC-78 "Bamboo Bomber" Some of the instructors were Bob Hodge, Evald Ely, Vern Thomas, Safe Ness. Bill Koski was the I.A. mechanic.

In 1947-48 there were 3 planes lost, 3 people killed. all were pilot error. error. I also had a mishap, and forced landed a Luscombe 8A N77657 in the trees on an iron ore dump in Leonidas, a very convenient location, as "Slicks" tavern was at the foot of the dump. I was at this time that a friend of mine showed up with three young ladies that were part of our regular group, and one of them that I had told earlier, to try to impress her with my daring do, that I had been involved in an airplane accident while in the service (I had witnessed one from the side lines) where an airplane blew a tire and flipped over. It was all B.S. and I had forgotten it, when she popped up and said, "Is that more that the accident you had when you were flying in the service". It was bad enough that some of the guys I chummed with looked at me like, what this? Someone later mentioned it to the press. Ya, it took awhile to live it down.

In 1947, Dec. I joined the Marine Corps reserve, so that I could accompany the reserve pilots to Duluth and Mpls to fly the with them in the reserve aircraft. Capt. Edwin Pachola swore me in on Dec. 3, 1947.

~~In 1949, I met and married my pretty bride Patricia "Patty Mae" Vlescini, we had ~~

In 1908 I went to work for the M.A. Hanna Co at the Douglas mine in Chisholm, and in the fall of that year, went to work for the Cleveland Cliffs Iron Co. at the Atkins mine in Kinney.

In 1949, I married a pretty lady I had met 2 yrs earlier, Patricia, "Pattie Mae" Vlescini. We had one son, Dan. Pushell ᵛˡᵉˢᶜⁱⁿⁱ

In 1950, Oct 11, I was re called to active duty, where the Korean war broke out. I knew my MOS would not guarantee me duty in an aviation unit, as I knew they needed replacements in the line Companies where lead poison was becoming a regular threat. I sat and discussed my immediate future with a corporal who looked like he had one hell of a hangover, he looked at me with a very red eyed, weary look, gave me a John Dillinger type smile and said, "What job would you like to have?" I thought

55

hey, they do recognize talent when they see it, I sat up straight and ~~thought~~ tried to sound like I was really on the ball, I suggested to him, it would be in the best interest of the U.S.M.C. and all concerned, if they were to assign me, a real hot shot, to a heavy equipment unit as an operator, dozer, shovel (which I still would not know how to operate) grader, even a truck, if all the other positions were already filled. He asked a few questions like, what grade completed, I didn't dare to tell him, I was struggling with the 8th grade when I quit, so I mumbled like 10th grade, "Sports?" sure, basketball, football, hell, he's never going to know, besides, what Marine didn't play football? I did do well in swimming, gymnastics

So, after more questions and answers, and several swigs of water, he was drinking from a quart size jar, he again smiled, says "this should take care of it, good luck", he folded the paper, put it in an envelope and told me to report to hut no. I believe it was, number 69, it should have been anyway, I reported to a slightly grey haired staff sgt., handed him the envelope, as he looked at the contents I asked, "Heavy equipment?" without looking up, he put it in typewriter, nodded, ticked away for 2 min., handed me the paper, said to me, the truck is loading at bldg 34 at 1000 hrs. motioning that I go right as I head out ~~through the~~ to the street. Walking toward the pick up area, I opened the envelope and peeked at the typing which was in large lettering, "Weapons Co. 2nd batt: Flamethrower Schooling, Tent camp 2". Well, it really was about the last thing I would have thought of ending up in, and bitterly so, it sure was heavy equipment, 70 lbs. It

It turned out the training was fun and interesting, we practiced with water and had some giant water gun fights. I was 20 yrs of age at this time. I also went thru a course in machine guns, neither of which I was assigned to when I got to Korea. We trained with tanks, aircraft holding close air support, and of course amphibious landings.

Left the States in Oct 1951 aboard a Victory Ship, U.S.S. Aiken Victory, ~~Deer~~ at Kobe Japan, we left our seabags and personal gear.

Arrived in Pusan Korea, were put on a train and brought north, detrained somewhere just south of the 38° parallel. Were put in trucks and driven farther north. Soon we could see debris lying alongside the road, which parallelled a river, there were smashed jeeps, trucks, artillery pieces, helmets, clothing, stretchers, and in the river, several bodies of Chinese + North Koreans were floating by. Soon we could hear our artillery and then we could see incoming rounds bursting in the area.

The trucks were halted and we were seperated, in alphabetical order, told of the units we were to join, and put in under command of an enlisted person, who displayed no rank, told to bring our gear and follow him. We climbed a long time up the side of this mountain, lying on the ground whenever a round sounded over our heads, or exploded within a half a mile of us, the person leading us just kept moving without ducking at all, soon some of us were in danger of being left behind in this hostile, soon to be dark country. When reaching our units we were assigned

To Whom It May Concern:

    I never considered myself a hero, in any sense of the word. I must admit that I was an extremely patriotic, flag waving, gung ho person, who was fascinated with the military, and the Marine Corps in particular. I would have preferred to have served in the capacity of aircraft pilot. It was not to be for me, because in short, I did not have the intelligence it required. I considered myself very fortunate to have at one time served in aviation as air crew and ground crew, and could have stayed in this field, had I chose to stay in the Corps as a regular.

    The Marine Corps was good to me, any trouble I had, I brought on myself, which was never anything serious. I knew that when I signed my name to the enlistment papers, I was subject to be called upon to perform in situations that would be injurious and life threatening. My main concern was, that if the situation did occur such as combat that I could make a good account of myself. I often thought what it would be like to be in a tight situation, where the odds may not be in my favor, to be wounded, and to purposely kill another individual.

    I remember well, my first combat experience, where I actually saw the enemy running at us from the front, and trying to flank us by using a large drainage ditch as cover. I remember the feeling of near panic when the bullets smacked into the trees above my head, and the splat sound they made when the guy to my left was hit in the chest. I remember the enemy falling when they were hit, and how nimble they were when they moved. I remember the sense of power, almost as tho I were indestructable when I fired my machine gun at them and saw them literally leave the ground in a cloud of dirt and dust when the bullets found home, I remember thinking to myself, Is this ever exciting, it's actually happening just like the movies, except you could not only see and hear this, you could smell it, the strong smell of cordite from the guns & grenades, the smell of garlic from the Chinese and the white phosphorous smoke, the smell of the dead from previous actions. I have to admit, I found some pleasure in the excitement, listening to the bullets whine when they ricochette, and always the sense of ~~power~~ indestructibility transfered to your body & brain by the power you could unleash with the ~~p~~ squeeze of a trigger.

I remember the helpless feeling when the person next to you is struggling to breath because the bullet fractured his chest, how we helped him by plugging the hole with our finger, only to see him go limp.

I remember looking at the Chinese ~~soldier~~ soldiers lying on the ground and their japanese rifles and bayonets were some times longer than their bodies, and how some of them appeared to be only 14-15 yrs of age.

I remember the incident on June 3 1951, when I and a Sgt Smith were caught in the open, while checking a series of bunkers, ~~the~~ we thought had been abandoned, when suddenly, 3 grenades went off right in front of us, and the machine gun within started firing, so close I could feel the muzzle blast, how I waited for them to concentrate on a target beyond us (I had the good fortune to find ~~a~~ a shallow shell hole) when they swung the gun to fire at guys coming up behind. I raised up to fire and my B.A.R. jammed, nothing happened! The guy feeding the belt into the machine gun, tapped the gunner on the arm and pointed to me, I thought, this is surly the end, he can't miss me from here 25 ft away, I decided laid as flat as I could and waited for the hammer like effect, the bullets have when they strike. Unbeknown to me, the gunner could not depress the gun to hit me and the rest of our unit coming up didn't allow them any time to work at it. So after a few ~~minutes~~ seconds of lying as still as I could, I realized that the bolt on the B.A.R. must be filled with dirt.

Joe Villoni

reading some of those statements given to reporters shortly after the action, makes me wonder if I were in the same action.

Bergren, has my original letter, from hospital in Japan. he was in batt hdqs at the time and asked me to send him in writting what happened that night, as he said, stressing, the crucial moments, that the colonel stated, their was a lack of wittness.

I had originally written to Bergren, when I was aboad hospital ship Repose in Pusan harbor, and told him that Joe should be recomended for M.OH.

When I wrote to Bergren, I purposly omitted my action with the Thompson, because I felt that it meght be conscrued that I was trying to take advantage of the situation for personal gain.

I have heard some of the accounts purposely given by colonel "Sliver Ass" Nyhart which seems to imply that he was shoulder to shoulder with the guys on the point; the truth is, he never left the area of the Batt hdqs, as I personally saw him there while I was recieving med aid. I did see him get knocked on his ass when a ~~30~~ struck the base of the tree he was standing on peering thru a pr of binoculars. Why he was awarded a Navy Cross for that action is an insult. Had he been in close as he should have been, he would not have allowed the pull back that took place, the evening of the 15th that laid the groundwork (no pun) for the gooks to occuppy the commanding ground in front of us.

On the other hand, I believe that most of the statements made were done so ~~to aid in the intent~~ with you in mind, but also provided some to get some ~~pullout~~ recognition for them selves

60

Also, the Colonel that told us, the night of Sept 13 while we attended a movie, who stated," Men! I do not know for sure where were going, or when were going, I only know there will be alot of purple hits, was, Colonel Warnham - not Nyhart.

I wrote most of this out for Donald Knox who was at the time writting a book on this action, and who was an excellent author, ~~but he~~ and I was in contact with him clearing up some of the statements I wrote and were not entirely clear, But Donald died and the person that completed the book did a very sloppy job, and ~~not accurate~~ more inaccurate. I suggested to Donald to change the language some, altho that is the language used at the time, it would have been better to abbreviate it.

~~On the 15TH of Sept, 1951   we~~

On the 14TH of Sept. 1951 about 10:00 AM, ~~shortly~~ 3 hrs or so after hearing gunfire and grenades down the line from my position, (we had ~~captured~~ taken a N.K. prisoner a bout 8:00 AM, he wanted to surrender.) I was informed by Contreas

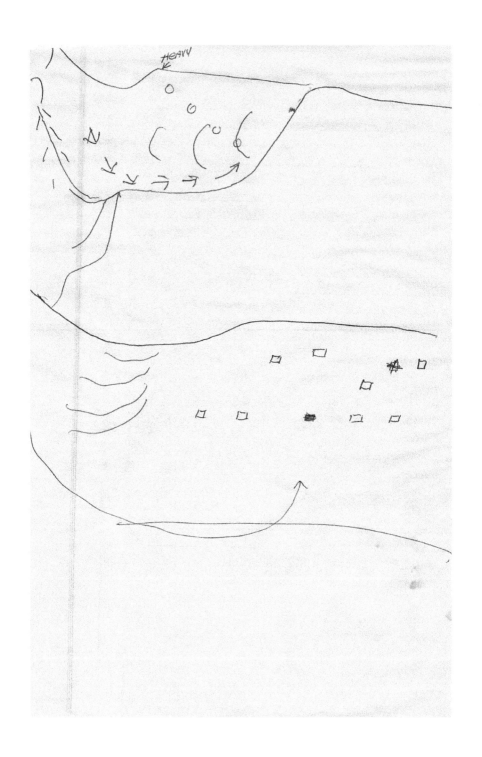

HEAVY

About 3:00 PM on Sept 14, whilst awaiting orders, we received a surprise attack from the wooded area to the N.W. of our position, it started with much gun & rifle fire and then several mortar rnds came in, one of which struck our corpsman, Earl May, in the legs & back, I believe in the head. I helped carry him out. That left us with no corpsman, as Hoover, the other corpsman was wounded while assisting 2 people who were injured by mines.

Contreras then assumed the duties of corpsman, on the morning of the 15th we found a N.K. soldier, who was setting about 15 yds in front of our position, I had just awakened and saw this guy setting there grinning and then waved to me. Many things went thru my mind for a few seconds, I thought he must have signaled an attack. After fumbling for my rifle and shouting a warning, several guns zeroed in on him and I shouted to Joe, there's a good setting hen. We ordered him forward, but had to wait for him to put his sneakers on first, which could have cost him. A short time later there was gun fire on the opposite side of the slope, some distance away

Later that morning, about 10:00 AM, I was standing on the slope of a hill, probably digging a hole. We spent alot time digging holes, when Contreras came up and with his mexican accent says, "Conway, you knew Lefty Gomez?" He then informed me that he was considered back in Omaha, a "desperado" type. Told me he was killed, showed to me a letter from Gomez to his mother, telling her not to grieve if he was killed, and that hopefully he would be awarded the M.O.H.

I wish to mention the following, only because I think it points to the politics involved in the awards + recommendations.

Shortly after I was able to use my right arm well enough to write, I wrote a letter to Ted Bergerson (SP) who had written to me asking me to detail the events of the night of Sept 15-16 concerning Joe Vittori and myself. I was still very much disturbed, constantly seeing in my mind Joe getting struck with that bullet, and my helplessness to do anything more than throw a grenade in response. I had been hit with grenade fragments in the head and face and shot in the right shoulder, I could see only with my right eye, was bleeding bad thru most of the fight, could throw grenade with my left arm and could barely pull the pins with my right hand.

When I wrote to ~~Bergeson~~ Bergeson, I purposely neglected to highlight some things I had done because I wanted Joe to be awarded the M.O.H. Not once thinking that I would ever be recommended for an award.

~~Imagine~~ Imagine my surprise, when a sgt, (cannot remember name) but he was paralyzed from waist down) whom I met in the hospital in Yokuska, told me, that sgt Xester had told him, ~~that too~~ that he had recommended both of us for M.O.H. My immediate response was, "There has to be a mistake". And on top of that, a letter from Bergerson stated, you too have been recommended for award.

Well, after giving it some thought, I figured the sgt, who was very much sedated, probably was mistaken, I never asked anyone, or mentioned it again, until I met sgt Xester at Camp Lejune N.C. and he personally told me he felt that Joe + I both should have ~~the~~ M.O.H. but was discouraged from recommending it being told — no two M.O.H. in same fox hole

Thurmon
Xester
Clark
3 yrs after
battle re-
wrote re.

1

Once upon a time, there was a parcel of land called, the Virginia Municipal Airport, it was constructed there by an organization called, the WPA under the administration of President Franklin D. Roosevelt, in a time when people were still willing to work with their backs and their hands ~~and were happy to re- ceive~~ when pay was poor, work was hard, spirits were even high, people were friendly. As Margaret Mitchel ~~would have put it~~, it was ~~a time~~ the last days of a world still at peace and believing they knew what direction ~~they~~ it was headed in, of men and women and women who were proud, pretty and adventuresome. Look for it now in the memories of ~~old~~ a few old men and fewer books, as it is truly gone forever. GONE WITH THE WIND It was during, the beautiful 1930's ~~USA~~ + 40's USA.

I can remember back to about 1936, seeing some of the old airplanes that frequented the field and hearing names of airplanes and men such as, Stinson Travel-Air, Norseman, cub, Aeronca Waco, Dusty Rhodes, Tisdell, Ween, Spehar, Nunamaw, Robey Bud Hill 1400 st.

The longest runway, stretched from ~~13th~~ 13st So, to just short of the So drive, where the Glenwood plant is now located, the shortest strip was the east-west that ran where the row of houses now sit along the So side of 30th st So. from the old D&P rail bed on the East, to the D&P property on the west. This runway was usually ~~used only~~ when the wind was pretty stiff from east or west. In the center of the field in concrete stabs were an arrow pointing north and the word VIRGINIA, painted white. ~~Standard were pastured~~ ~~rabbits~~ and abounding with wildlife, partridge so and ~~rabbit~~ in such numbers you could sometime get some with sling shot, a favorite place for the hawks and —

It was generally kept clear of tall — city crews who would keep the by citizens who would with hand scythe keep the verge of the grass cut to feed their cows & horses. There were hazel nuts and currant bushes galore in the wooded parts of the field.

One the east side of the field, where the city garage is now located, there were one or two, small, poorly constructed hanger type buildings (the term, hanger comes from the early days of aviation when they would literally hang the balloons and aeroplanes from the ceilings.) There was the typical city constructed bldg called, the "city shack" which was much like the shanties shacks of the era. In that building was stored, a desk a stool, a toilet and some benches, on the walls the usual calendars & notes, some pin up type pictures of pretty gals & aeroplanes.

An airport superintendant and 5 or 6 elderly men that were referred to as airport guards who wore badges to tell, that I remember, Clyde Lemore was the sup. and I believe there was also an assistant sup. Names of some of the guards were Olivin Prince, who were an especionally easy going person and liked to have company, and was always good to the kids, some of the other guys were gruff but good guys, there was Patty McGuire, Tony Matckuvich an efe prize fighter, they worked 3 shift. We used to get a kick out of Some of these guys were w.w.1 and Spanish am. war vets, they were suffering and the usual ailments of old age and we kids would get a kick out of their telling us of experiences they had as young men, when suddenly in the middle of a story, they would reach over and pick up the phone and shout, "air port "airport" when the phone had not rang and at other times the phone would ring until you told them to ans. etc, or we would suddenly stall to one, I have an airplane there, not to be caught unaware they would say "

66

3

thought I heard a plane, and we would go outside, they would mostly shine a flashlight into the sky and say, I can hear it, but I can't see it.

The city shack was also a check point for the law officer who would make a call to the station from there, one I remember well, was abe collins, who always carried a german luger pistol and with a little prompting, we would set up a target a couple [150] ft out or so and he would show us how well the pistol fired, this was not considered out of the ordinary at the time as there were always people hunting birds on the airport. It was not uncommon in that era for citizens to blast a varment that might be after their chickens or other live stock, every one had cows, horses, chickens, ducks, pigs all at the time. I remember well, people blasting stumps and rocks with dynamite to dig basements.

It seems now almost ridiculous to have had 7 or 8 people fully employed to watch a patch of land that for the most part was maintained to handle maybe 20 air planes landing and leaving per yr and during the first part of war II the army sent a squad of HOME GUARD here to guard that pea patch.

We, as kids found it facinating, whenever a plane was using the field. I remember about 1934, I remember the ford Tri-motor and the bi planes doing stunts as they acrobatic maneuvers were then called, I remember a girl walking on the wing of the plane and a parachuter who had 3 chutes fail "and finally coming to earth with a 3rd chute. seeing them pick up a handkerchief from the ground with a wing tip. and in about 1938, the Auto gyro (Petairin) that did anything but go straight up & down, in fact the pilot I'm sure was greatly

67

crouching the
actor to store

Oliver shows
Bailey Mill
with arrow
point No

water tank
was name
all helped pilot
check route

barred when it got off after a very long run.

People were able to ride in the t.m. motor for paying a penny a pound per person, and the Phillips Oil Co. always had an aeroplane once or twice a year would go up and sky write "Phillips Co.", usually in the evening when the air was calm at about 8 Thous. ft.

During those years of the 30's thru 40's it was the custom to have the name of the town painted in large letters on the water tanks of each town and across the tops of roofs of large buildings. I remember Bailey Mill and the Recreation bldg had "Virginia" with an arrow pointing north in large yellow letters, ther was very helpful to aviators back then when all you had to navigate with was a magnetic compass and a line drawn on a road map. Many a time I have gone down low enough to get the number of the hwy I was following, or to follow the rail road like was called, flying the iron compass. On a nice clear cold day you could see smoke from indust. chimneys for 50 miles, such as the paper plants in International Falls, or Cloquet. Or coming up from Mpls or Wisc., see the sunlite reflecting off the Oil storage tanks at Wrenshal, or see Duluth show up on the hill side as a white area

1939 to 1943 are quite hazey to my memory of the airport, as we moved from Redwood over during that period, there was an airshow in 1940. I remember the airplanes flying over Mt Iron performing aerobatics and dropping leaflets advertising the show. and what a thrill it was when an old bi-plane came down and buzzed me as I was standing in a field waveing to the plane, I never forgot how thrilld I was to have received that attention and you

5

later, I would, when I could, do the same for some
kid I would see waving from a lonesome spot in
the country side, especially if these were girls waving.

About 1943, the war going big, and occasionally
one of the hometown pilots would bring a military plane up
this way and buzz off the town. There were several I
remember well, but probably the most memorable was
when Wayne Conners buzzed the town with a big beautiful B-17, it was about noon on a beautiful sum-
mer day, I can still see and hear that old bomber.
Jerry Simon who lived on 1st st. in Ridgwood used to
really grease the town, and would open the bomb bay
doors of the B-25 and drop a message to his mother.
A pilot who I do not now remember his name had
a B-13 and landed here for a few hrs. and when
he left, I asked him if he could go between the 2
smoke stacks at the water + light plant, and the son-
of-a-gun did it!

One evening, about dusk, in Aug or so, in 1944
we lived on the north end of the airport, on 13 st. So.
when suddenly there was a light, shinning thru the
window of the house and a terrific roar as an airplane
also a B-13 Navy version SNV roared over the houses
and then came back again and again, at first I
thought it was some military pilot just having
fun, but soon I realized the guy was looking for the
runway, I also knew what to do about it, grabbing a couple of fuses (my father was a RR brake-
man) I started to run toward the end of the runway but the plane had disapeared, once again, I
thought it was just a buzz job. About an hour
later, we heard on the radio or thru a phone call,
that an army plane crashed on the levie by the
Evelath dump, actually it was a Navy Trainer, the
pilot had flown over his home area North of U

6

and become disorientated and ran the plane out of gas,
he tried to land it on the hwy, but there was too much
traffic, then engine quit so he set it down alongside
the road amongst some large boulders, and struck the
road going to the Eveleth City dump, flipped it on its
back and miraculously survived practically unscathed. He
was heard to say while standing there by the wreck, "Well,
I'm a seaman 2nd class now."

70

Old Airport

a Bill P. Pontenen flew a P-38 over the town and did a few slow rolls, Art B. Tormey flew a B-29. Those were great things for the people up on the Iron Range, as we rarely saw there airplanes. And the time a B-17 landed at Virginia and became bogged down in the muskeg, that was 1949.

B-17 landed 49

Jack Morman

There was the time that I was flying with a guy name Ed Strick, Ed had been discharged early when he parachuted into a drainage ditch and broke his back, so he learned to fly as a civilian, we were flying a taylorcraft airplane in 1945, it was a cloudy day, so we headed for a blue hole in the clouds and got up topside and when we came down thru cloud about 10 min later, we did not know where we were at, it was hazey and we could not see any distance, tho we were quite concerned about finding a familiar landmark, we found first, something far more appealing, 2 girls standing in front of a house alongside a gravel road (as most roads were then) and waving to us, without a second thought, down wing, down nose, come around left, line up and buzz right over there heads as impressive as a 65 horse taylorcraft can be, add throttle, pull nose up and the damned eng. quit, cold!, as the old saying goes, "There we were", Ed, was busy not to get excited, and certainly not one to let a pretty girl think he couldn't handle that kite, lined up with the road, went under a telphone wire power wires, made a beautiful landing, right in front of the house and the girls, the only 2 things that went wrong were that we struck the mail box, and the two girls ran into the house. Within minutes cars were lining the rd, a deputy Shreff showed up and cleared enough cars away so we could take off. It turns out we were over the Makinen area.

Heres one that may be hard to believe, but I swear its the truth, I believe it was in the spring of 44 of 44? there was alot of snow, two fairly husky guys were flying in an Aronca chief side by side 65 hp coats, I and one other kid, al

every dream day abt of sno

my age, 14-15 were walking thru the sno out on the field watching their plane taxiing back + forth on the So east No west runway, trying to pack down the snow (skied) and tried 2 or 3 times to get their overloaded little plane off the ground, ~~seeming~~ not seeming to care about the eng. heating up, finally they got up enough speed to lift the plane from the snow, heading So east, suddenly, the wing dropped and out comes a person, arms flailing trying to stay up right, the plane, about 30 ft in the air, continued to bank left, as the nose dropped, and actually were inverted and plowed into the sno and willow brush, we ran over to the wreck, the airplane was damaged, but covered with sno, by the time we got there, the person that had jumped, was helping the other guy out, and was repeating over + over, didn't you hear me tell you to jump, I don't know what happened, I couldn't control it. As it turned out, they were not injured, except the guy that jumped, had some cuts on his face from landing in the willow brush, the deep snow certainly saved them both. & hey picked up there gear, they were going hunting somewhere, we helped them get over to the city shack, where the guard was playing solitaire and completly oblivious of what had taken place, the two guys, called a taxi cab 30 mi away and went to the Ormond Hotel. The airplane laid out there for a couple of months—

And there was the big tall guy, named Ray, who, Comes after Ray Woods trial → as was the custom, primed the eng. and turned the swith to both, but apparently did not check the throttle of the little Luscombe, walked to the front, pulled the propeller thru to start it and it really come to life, Ray was alone at the time except for a man and women who out of curiosity were attentively watching, as the airplane started forward, with enough power on it appeared to have left the ground, Ray grabbed the wing struts and acting as a pivot held on while the airplane started going in circle

showing and
newspaper +
toilet paper

Buzzed out her
took license

progressively faster + faster and Ray was shouting to the couple to grab the airplane, do something to help, they stood there fixed, unable to comprehend the meaning. About that time, my brother Larry and myself drove up alongside the building, we saw the couple standing as the mesmerized, but until we got out of the car we knew nothing was wrong, suddenly we could hear shouting and hear the engine running and soon we saw a silver Luscombe go by at a pretty high rate of speed, about this time Ray was becoming exhausted and could not have held on much longer, we realized the situation immediately, I grabbed on to the tail and was dragging alongside, and it did slow the plane down but it also added more weight than Ray could hold in one place, Larry was running alongside trying to open the door to get at the switch, and for a minute or so, the situation was in doubt, but we managed.

And there was the incident involving the same taylorcraft airplane that we had forced landing in Maltineu. As it turned out, this airplane was a true jinx. Anyway, the guy flying it was Ray the mayor of one of the range cities, the plane was owned ~~and rented~~ by Vern Thomas, the instructor was a former Navy pilot, with whom I was standing alongside at the time, watching Ray shoot landings, the airplane it seems had a habit of losing power, if the throttle was advanced too quickly, and while landing with skiis, on the snow, two or three landings, Ray applied power, to go around again but the engine died. the plane came to a stop. The instructor had a pr of sno shoes and was going to go out to assist Ray, when Ray, dressed like an Escomo squeezed out of the plane - It always looked as tho the plane was giving birth to some big furry entity when one exited with all the furs on. And Ray, walked to the front of the plane, grabbed the prop, give it a pull, the eng at full power, jumped to life, forcing Ray to dive away from the prop, and headed so with al-

73

solully, no one at the controls, the airplane, empty, promptly lifted into the air, while all of us stood gaping and wondering, now what? The airplane, slightly nose high started a gentle left turn as the wind was slightly from So. west turned thru almost 180° and was headed for the populated area of Virginia, fortunately, the slight tail wind caused the plane to slowly pitch nose down and then gradually the dive steepened and the plane turned slightly left went almost straight into the brush, where the ~~with from~~ snare motors is now situated, again 3-4 ft of snow and willow brush cushioned the impact and the plane was ~~re-buildable~~ re-usable. At the time none of us were thinking of anything other than to be thankful it didn't slam into a house. The plane was in fact re-~~buildable~~ usable by Bill Martilla, and still held more surprises

Jack Morman Bill this plane in

Bill Kishi Evelet Ely

Youngest private pilot in minn 1947 - 17 yrs old

Well, during the war years, it was always exciting when ~~the~~ a home town military pilot would fly over the city with a bomber or a fighter, ~~some~~ some of them I remember, were Wayne Conners, Bill Portinen, Art Thomer, Maj Volcanier and Col Tapp, both from Eveleth, Elwood Young, Lyle McCabe, and some others from this area who I did not know, I believe that had every time one of them flew over the town the enlistments went up.

After the war, everyone who wanted a job, had one, in fact for several years, a guy couldn't go into a bar to have a beer without a foreman for some contractor coming into the bar ask if you wanted to go to work, often offering to pay time and a half for a week or so. Everyone was living comfortably and all the veterans had the G.I. bill and many of them who were comfortable with the jobs they had, decided to take flying lessons. There were three or four independent flight instructor at the old airport who were attempting to start up flying schools

74

hunted rabbits and porkatoes on the airport, and even through out town, if a varmint was after someones chickens they would blast it with a .410, I remember many times seeing people blast rocks loose with dynamite when digging a ditch or basement.

It seems now almost rediculous to have had 7 or 8 people part time employed to watch over a piece of land that had never be 30 airplanes a year coming and going, and the army sent a squad of soldiers here complete with rifle, belts & bayonetts to guard this pea patch.

and even more rediculous was the civilian airplane spotters perched in the dome of city hall looking for, axis aircraft that might be approaching over fair city - that wasnt a carrier airplane in the world that could patrol beyond 350 miles from base. - But I guess it gave people a feeling of contribution to the war effort.

There was a pilot with a bi plane who used to frequent our airport, and go up in the evening and sky-write as it was called, by running corvus oil, a light grade oil that is used in electric.
into the exhaust collector ring and smoke would emit from it and they would write "Phillips 66". I believe his name was Carl Goebbels

In the 30s-30s-40s it was customary to have the name of the town written on the tops of buildings and on the sides of water tanks, with an arrow pointing no. The rec building and Baileys Mill had such - was a great aid to dead reconing now. - some cities like Intion nal. Falls, Cloquet and Grand Rapids - you could see the smoke and steam from the paper mills from 50 mi out - and you could sure smell it once you got into it.

1939-1943 are quite hazy in my memory because we moved to Mt. Iron area and I had to hitchhike to Va.

Another incident I'll always remember, in 1940, they had an airshow in Va and there were 3 biplanes over the Mt Iron area throwing leaflets out advertising the show, and doing some aerial maneuvers, I was standing out in the pasture when one of the planes flew over and I waved, the pilot could clearly be seen looking over the side of the plane and winged the airplane over and dove straight at me, really dressing me off, what a thrill, to have been given that attention - ever after, when I was flying, and would see kids waving in some lonesome out of the way place, I would buzz them and wave, and especially if there were pretty girls waving.

Some of the names of pilots and plane owners from the 30s 1940s.

Art Goebel, Norman Terdahl, Noel Wein, Barney Barnard, Dusty Rhodes - Ernie Metcalf, Thunder Johnson, Clinton Siegel, Speed Holman, Betty Coates, Bud Hill, Bill Nancarrow, Dewie Thomas, Doc Saviff, Bill Odegaard, John Siverson, Jack Robig, Shack Spelar (welder/mech) Nilo Latvalla, Bill Odegard

words pilot jumped from plane
'44-'45

Bud Hill 1938 Stinson his auto
1944-45 airplane, Woods - Joke Ness - could took off by self.
Ray C. Holding Sexcomb, going over circles.

Former Army Pilot, looking at the girls leave the fence taxied PT-19 into another PT 19. - severe wing damage

22 losses in spin from 6,000 ft.
lost license for 30 days + buzzing Pallele house
landed near Makinen - Walter came over. Ed Linch

I would like to submit this memory in writing on behalf of my friend of many years, who was a flight instructor and president of Northeast airways inc. of Virginia Minn. in the late 40 and early 50's and who was always willing to give his time and advise to a 17 yr old who was in need of a lot of guidance.

Ray Glumak, having served in the Naval aviation as a pilot, often had been assigned to fly close air and air support missions for the Marine Corps, of which service I served in, thus we were bonded by a common respect of each others duties, and our personalities seemed to mesh

As best I can remember it, I would like to relate an incident that took place, nearly 50 yrs ago. I think this is a good time to share this, with Ray at this time being bestowed one of the highest honors that can be awarded to an aviator, the Minnesota Aviation Hall of Fame.

There was an era, in the 1940's that hunting and trapping wolves for a 35.⁰⁰ bounty was considered profitable and nessasary and one of the most sporting ways to hunt them was with the light high wing airplanes equiped with skis, so it was, that many pilots carried with them a carbine type rifle in the plane when flying in the northern parts of Minn. and it certainly was fortunate for one person, that Ray was looking down at the ice for signs of wolves on this particular day, in fact for these particular few minuts, as it was life or death in that short of time.

As I remember it, Ray Glumak was flying a passenger north of Virginia, into the Crab Lake area on a day that was 40° late in the day with dark only 40 min. or so away. Going down

Which proved in this instance to be a blessing, for at least one individual.

Ray was flying with a student in the area of Pine Lake, the temperature was -35° and late afternoon, when they spotted what appeared to be a wolf crossing the ice. Thinking this would be a good time to bag this critter and still have time to retrieve it before dark, they swung around to come between the island and the wolf. Crossing over this ice at low altitude and preparing to fire, they could suddenly see this was a person, and obviously in dire need of help, stumbling and flailing about in the snow. It was obvious with darkness setting in, there was ~~but one~~ no choice of what to do if this person was to survive. Land! Now!

Ray landed, looked to the person who stumbled to the door of the plane, obviously in advanced stages of hypothermia, incoherent and losing coordination, altho in this state he still recognized Ray. Ray could not at first make who this person was because of him being covered with frost and ice, but soon recognized him as Melton Rocke, a former flight student and owner of a resort on Lake Vermilion. Also he was a novice trapper who had flown his Aronca Champ ~~airplane~~ on an earlier that morning to check his mink traps on Crab Lake and discovered he could not get his airplane started after it had sat for close to two hours, and realizing he was in serious trouble, and becoming very chilled, he started walking through the snow and wooded area to Pine Lake, and had covered about 5 miles before late in the day, he fell through the ice in a creek soaking one leg of his leather flight suit to the hip. After several unsuccessful attempts to start a fire with just a book of matches, he began to realize that he probably too would not make it through the night, and in desperation started across the ice.

It had to be a case of a prayer being answered, to see that little silver airplane zoom by out of nowhere and see it swing into the wind and land.

The student refused to wait on the ice while Ray flew Milton to his home, so again, there was no choice only one way to do it. Stuff Milton, who was slight of build on top of the student and squeeze his own 6'4" frame into the cabin. And with what had to be a superb example of airmanship, get that little 65 horse Luscombe into the air on a very small lake. With Rays many years of flying experience, and that little Luscombe performing as if it too realized the desperation of the situation, Ray managed to get Milton to his home on Sunset island, where he was to spend many happy years. To the relief of a very very grateful Milton Rockie, as he would never have survived much longer on the ice.

Respectfully,
Deb Conaway

Lyle and his wife Patricia

LYLE CONAWAY

To the tune of "Drinking Rum and Coca-Cola"

Chinese railroad ride in style, 44 hours go one mile,
Chinese think this fast indeed.
Blow up tracks, slow down speed.

Drinking soda, beer and vodka... *(fading)*

Chinese girls in little white shoes.
Smoke your butts and drink your booze.
Got no cherry but that's no sin,
They got the box that it came in.

Drinking soda, beer and vodka.
No mama, no papa.
No flight pay can draw.
Hey Joe, wanna old kum-sha.

Semper Fi

ABOUT THE AUTHOR

Lyle Conaway, having no birth certificate, enlisted in the US Marine Corps in December 1945 at the age of 15 years 7 months while claiming to be 16—soon to be 17. The Veterans Administration recognizes service beginning through December 31, 1946 as World War II, thus Lyle qualified as a veteran of WWII. He was transported from San Diego to Hawaii on the USS Shangri-La, and then flew across the Pacific Ocean on VMR 533. The transport brought Lyle to Johnston Island, Kwajalein in the Marshall Islands, Guam, and, after joining a Marine transport unit, flew on to Tsingtao, China. He spent eight months at Nanyuan Airfield in Peiping (now Beijing), and then returned to Hawaii aboard a merchant ship in April 1947 for an early discharge due to military cutbacks.

On December 20, 1947, Lyle enlisted for four years in the US Marine Corps Reserve, an inactive reserve that permitted flying with pilots over Duluth and Minneapolis, MN, which occurred three times over his span in the reserves. By October 1950, he was called back to active duty in the infantry which brought him to Korea. The rest is history; a story basically about Joe Vittori and Lyle in Korea highlighting the dates September 15–16, 1951.

The story of Hill 749 is told from the perspective of one of the survivors. It was an intense time for a young marine with a gung-ho attitude who soon became tired of war.

www.mcafdn.org

"The safest place in Korea was right behind a platoon of Marines. Lord, how they could fight!"
—MG Frank E. Lowe, USA, 1952

507-538-6669

Katie

CPSIA information can be obtained
at www.ICGtesting.com
Printed in the USA
BVHW032206251021
619851BV00004B/54